MW00390119

How to Play Erhu, the Chinese Violin

– the Full Version

H.H. Lee

A guide to playing erhu, the Chinese violin at home by yourself

How to Play Erhu, the Chinese Violin - the Full Version, Edition 1.0

Copyright © 2018 by H. H. Lee

All rights reserved. No part of this publication may be reproduced, distributed, or transmitted in any form or by any means, including photocopying, recording, or other electronic or mechanical methods, without the prior written permission of the publisher, except in the case of brief quotations embodied in critical reviews and certain other noncommercial uses permitted by copyright law.

ISBN: 9781980538769

Table of Contents

Preface

The erhu, also called the Southern Fiddle, is a two-stringed musical instrument that evolves from the xiqin (奚琴) played by the barbarian tribes (胡人) to the north of ancient China.　The Chinese name of the erhu literally means "an instrument of the *Hu* peoples that consists of two strings."　Commonly known as the Chinese violin in the West, the erhu belongs to the bowing family[1] in the modern Chinese orchestra[2]. The popularity of the erhu, irrespective of solo or ensemble, is largely attributed to its unique timbre that resembles human voices.

Members of the bowing family

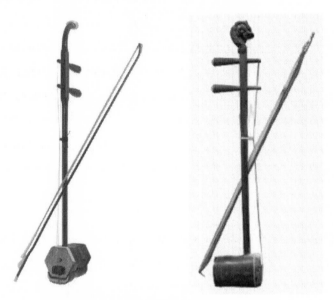

Erhu/二胡 (left) and Gaohu/高胡 (right)

---

[1]　The bowing family mainly consists of erhu, gaohu (high-pitched erhu) and zhonghu (middle-pitched erhu), as well as gehu and banhu sometimes.

[2]　The modern Chinese orchestra consists of four families, namely the bowing (bowed string), plucking (plucked string), blowing (wind) and hitting (percussion).

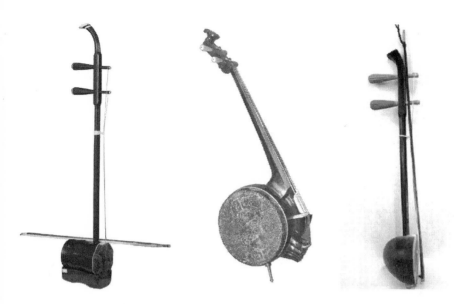

Zhonghu/中胡 (left), Gehu/革胡 (middle) and Banhu/板胡 (right)

Since the famous Chinese musician LIU Tianhua[3] drastically reformed the erhu structure in the early 1900s, numerous songs have been composed for both erhu solo and ensemble. Modifications to the erhu structure have been subsequently made in an attempt to improve the timbre and volume of sound. In the 1950s, the erhu started to serve as the mainstay of modern Chinese orchestras, assuming a similar role to the violin.

In the following, I will show you how to play the erhu. Even if you are an amateur of Chinese music, you can still play some simple songs with enough efforts. Remember, practice makes perfect! But the first thing to do, of course, is to choose a suitable erhu.

---

[3] LIU Tianhua/劉天華 (1895-1932), father of the modern erhu, was a Chinese musician and composer commended for using new materials to make erhu strings and tuning them on the basis of five positions (把位).

The above picture shows a modern Chinese orchestra of a small scale (less than the normal establishment of 60 members), in which the erhus (to the right) play a role similar to the violins in Western orchestras.

The Structure of the Erhu

An understanding of the erhu structure is the prerequisite of everything. The parts of an erhu are therefore illustrated in the following diagram:

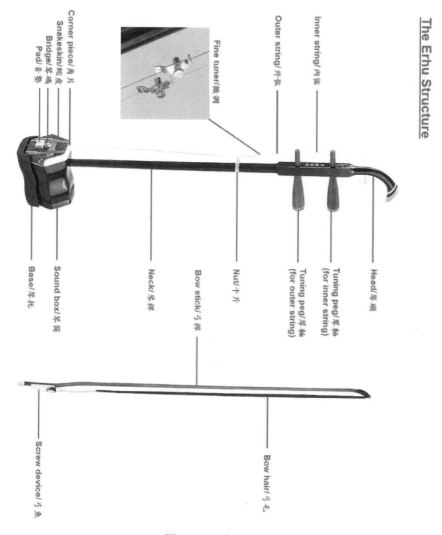

The parts of an erhu

Unless otherwise stated, most parts are made of wood. Their respective functions are described as follows:

Head/琴頭

The head does not serve any concrete purposes save for decoration. There are many forms of carved heads for the erhus like horse, ruyi, bat, phoenix, lotus, etc.[4], among which the crescent and dragon heads are the most popular forms.

Tuning pegs/琴軸

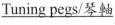

The tuning peg looks like a cone with a small hole at the end for the string to pass through and coil up on it. The two pegs are 7.5 cm apart from each other, 12 cm from the head and 50 cm from the sound box. We use them to adjust the tension on the strings to vary the pitches (the higher the tension, the higher the pitch).

Strings/弦

As its name implies, the erhu (the Chinese character *er*/二 means two) has two strings, viz. the inner string/內弦 (nearer to the player and usually tuned at D4) and outer string/外弦 (farther to the player and usually

---

[4] You may refer to the link: http://blog.xuite.net/hu.to/erhu/18547949-風「琴」萬種——琴頭之美, which showcases a variety of erhu heads.

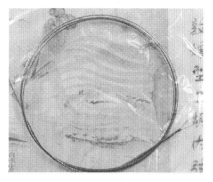

tuned at A4). They were made of silk in the past, but steel is used today because of its durable and tough nature. Also, steel produces clearer and more delicate sound. The inner string is thicker than the outer string, as it produces notes of lower pitches.

Neck/琴桿

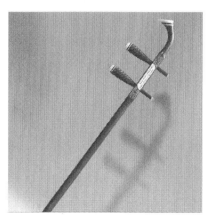

The neck is a long cylinder of wood (around 83 cm in length typically) that connects the head, tuning pegs, sound box and base together to form the erhu, as well as provides a supporting pillar for the left hand to move up and down in pressing the strings. Its cross sectional shape is preferably oval rather than circular to facilitate performance and resist bending.

Nut/千斤

The nut has often been made of several rings of string, but a metal or plastic hook is getting more prevalent, which can withstand palm sweat and clasp the strings more securely. Its main function is to define the vibrating lengths (scale lengths) of the open strings along with the bridge.

The sound box consists of a resonance body (13 cm in length) with one end wrapped up by the snakeskin (a diameter of 8.8 cm) and the other end covered by a wooden window (a diameter of 8 cm). String vibrations transmitted from the bridge to the snakeskin are amplified in the hollow sound box and then emitted through the window. The wooden window is always carved with decorative patterns or even Chinese characters that may be the crafter's surname or those bearing auspicious meaning.

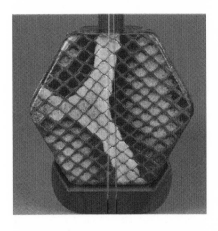

Snake skin/蛇皮

The snakeskin is either obtained from *Colubridae* (<0.3 mm in thickness) or *Pythonidae* (thickness between 0.3 and 1.0 mm). Inasmuch as most python species are protected under the CITES, only those bred in capacity will be used now, and alternatives like PET Polyester Membrane have been invented, which can also amplify the string vibrations and retain the unique flavor of the timbre.

Corner piece/角片

The corner piece is a sacrificial device that protects the top-right corner of the snakeskin against abrasion with the bow hair. Made of tortoiseshell in the past, they are now made of plastic or cow horn for the sake of the environment.

Bridge/琴碼

The trapezoidal bridge (8 mm in height, with the bottom's diameter being 14 mm) is usually made of maple with a small hole in the middle and two grooves at the top that hang the strings. It helps to transmit the string vibrations to the snakeskin and then the sound box. Along with the nut, it defines the vibrating lengths (scale lengths) of the open strings.

Pad/音塾

The pad, either made of a piece of cloth, felt or sponge, is inserted into the space between the strings and the snakeskin just beneath the bridge to absorb and minimize wolf tones[5].

---

[5] A wolf tone sounds like the howling of a wolf. When we play a note whose frequency matches the natural resonating frequency of the erhu, an artificial overtone will be produced. The original note will then be amplified due to constructive interference, and resulting in a wolf tone. Wolf tones should be eliminated at all as they are cacophonous in nature.

Base/琴托

The base is around 13.1 cm in length, 1.5 cm in thickness and 5.5 cm (front) / 5 cm (rear) in width.   Affixed at the bottom with screws and sometimes even embedded with lead, its main function is to stabilize the erhu by acting as the center of gravity and provide a smooth surface for the erhu to rest on the left thigh.

Bow hair/弓毛

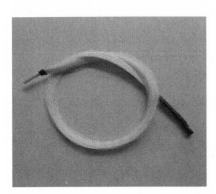

The bow hair is made of 240 to 250 horsehairs, each of which is 90 cm in length, with a diameter between 0.161 and 0.198 mm.   Unlike the violin, the bow hair of the erhu is always sandwiched between the inner and outer strings, moving to and fro to cause vibrations.

Bow stick/弓桿

The bow stick (85 cm in length) is made of an elastic bamboo attached with the bow hair.   We can use it to vibrate the outer strin) when playing certain songs like *Galloping War Horses*/戰馬奔騰 and *The Red Army Men Coming Back*/紅軍哥哥回來了.

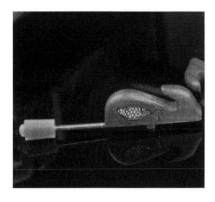

Screw device/弓魚

Either made of white jade, ivory or plastic, the adjustable screw device fixes the bow hair at the bow frog. Its Chinese name literally means "bow fish" because it looks akin to a fish, though different patterns like the eye/gill/scale of a fish also exist.

Fine tuners/微調

The metal fine tuners are installed on both strings to help us tune them by a small extent, such that we can accurately reach the right pitch without frequently twisting the tuning pegs, thus minimizing the damage done to the neck and tuning pegs.

Note: the measurements of the above parts are approximations only and actual figures may vary a bit.

We have looked into different parts of the erhu in detail, and can now learn to choose a good erhu on the basis of what we have learnt in this chapter so far.

How to Choose an Erhu

The quality of every musical instrument is dependent on three factors, namely material, craftsmanship and timbre. On the part of erhus, wood is the principal material and thus plays a vital role. The qualities of wood species, so as their prices, go down from the best and most expensive red sandalwood (*Pterocarpus santalinus*), the next-best aged red wood, to black wood and followed by red wood (the words black and red here refer to the species instead of the colors).

A red sandalwood erhu

An aged red wood erhu

A black wood erhu

Red sandalwood is no doubt the best, but too expensive due to its rarity. The price usually amounts to about USD3000. Aged red wood, though ranked the second in term of its quality, can also be very pricey if they are obtained from the remains of old furniture fabricated in the Ming or Qing Dynasties.

I recommend buying an erhu made of red wood at a price below USD100 for an amateur, since it is already sufficient for us to play a lot of songs with it satisfactorily. Of course, you can purchase a black wood erhu, which is certainly better in all aspects, if you are not on a tight budget.

On a par with the material used, the craftsmanship is equally important. The first step is to identify the place of origin, which is grouped under three Chinese cities: Beijing, Shanghai and Suzhou. Acoustically, Beijing's erhus are more sonorous, Shanghai's erhus are relatively softer, and Suzhou's erhus are a mixture of them. For this reason, I suggest buying a Suzhou's erhu for its balance in performance.

Thereafter, let us examine different parts of the erhu in detail, and start with the irreplaceable parts (the sound box, snakeskin and tuning pegs):

The sound box has many shapes, which can be hexagonal, octagonal, round, oval, or hybrids of these types. The hexagonal (prevailing in Southern China) and octagonal (prevailing in Northern China) types are the traditional ones with respective edges: the octagonal one generates louder sounds thanks to its larger volume; meanwhile the hexagonal one generates sweeter sounds thanks to better reflection. If you buy an erhu from a music store or from the Internet, you will probably come across the hexagonal one.

The hexagonal erhu   The octagonal erhu

Erhus with sound boxes in other shapes are modern modifications in a bid to improving sound amplification, and as a result they all generate louder and more solid sounds, particularly in the high-pitch regions (4th to 5th positions) without losing the original favor of erhus. However, the full potential of these kinds of erhus cannot be realized unless players have mastered the bowing skills, so you should think twice and take into account the pros and cons of different types of erhus before making the purchase.

The oval erhu   A hybrid (octagonal and oval) erhu

The snakeskin is part of the sound box responsible for the unique erhu sound, and thus we ought to pay special attention to it. A fine snakeskin should be bright in color, smooth in texture, moderate in thickness with its scales equally distributed, and even better if the scales are conspicuous and clearly distinguished from each other. You can touch the snakeskin too to feel its texture aside from using naked eyes only. In addition, the more and larger the yellow scales are, the better the quality of the snakeskin is.

As for the tuning pegs, they can either belong to the wooden (traditional) or mechanical gear type. From my point of view, the mechanical gear type is better because it helps to grasp the string, which will hardly be out of tune then. Moreover, it allows fine adjustment of pitch that the wooden type will otherwise require the fine tuners to do so. In this respect, amateurs should try to pick an erhu with tuning pegs of the mechanical gear type.

Mechanical gear-typed tuning pegs

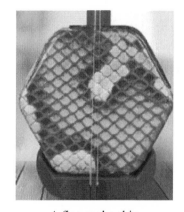
A fine snake skin

On top of these, we should also check the replaceable parts that affect the timbre to a considerable extent, since it is not desirable to replace them soon after the erhu is bought. The parts concerned are the nut, bridge and bow.

String has been used for typing the nut for a long period of time owing to its cheap cost and convenience, yet it is prone to break after becoming mildewed. To save the big effort at typing a new nut, we can use string treated with wax or even replace it with a plastic or metal hook, which can endure longer.

Recently, a movable nut has been invented to lower the pitches of the open strings from D4/A4 to G3/D4, whereby extending the range of the erhu by 4 tones at most. This device is not readily installed on erhus directly sold by manufacturers, but is really useful for more experienced players on certain occasions.

Being the medium through which string vibrations are transmitted to the snakeskin, the bridge has a big influence on the timbre of the erhu despite its comparably small size. Various types of bridges for different kinds of erhus are tabulated as follows:

Type of erhus	With loose snakeskin and dull sound	Common type in normal status	With tight snakeskin and bright sound

Wood species suitable for making the bridges	Red sandalwood, aged red wood, black wood, maple wood, pine wood, Ceylon ebony wood, or bamboo	Maple wood, especially those fried with oil[6]	Maple wood, especially those fried with oil; aged red wood, pine wood or fragrant rosewood
Ideal physical properties	Highly dense and hard; slim and long; small at the bottom and flat at the top; with bigger holes but shallower grooves	Soft but tough	Lowly dense and soft; fat and short; large at the bottom; with smaller holes but deeper grooves

The final task is to choose a suitable bow. A fine bow should have a straight stick with few knots and even in thickness (a diameter ranging from about 0.65 to 0.8 cm), while its hair should be ideally made of white horsehair and abundant in number. White horsehair has evenly-distributed scales that can attract the rosin powder more rigidly, by which it can vibrate the strings better. When examining the bow, we have to check that if the hair is combed neatly and affixed to the end of the stick (frog) securely lest the hair would detach from the stick soon after the bow is used.

Besides, length and weight also have a significant impact on our control

---

[6] Oil frying is a process of frying the bridge with vegetable oil, rosin and paraffin wax to remove the moisture and organic extractives in the wood, and fill the vessels that are left empty with rosin and paraffin wax, whereby chemically changing the nature of the bridge. The space in the wood cells will also be expanded, which enhances the transmission of vibrations and hence the effectiveness of the bridge. An erhu equipped with a bridge fried with oil has brighter and mellower sound than others.

of the bow. Generally speaking, a heavier bow with a length of 85 cm that renders a sense of gravity is deemed fitting for most players.

Although most of the criteria for choosing a good erhu have been mentioned, it is still difficult for amateurs to find one on their own. In this regard, when you are about to buy an erhu, ask your teacher or an experienced player to accompany you to a music store, where you can personally hear the sounds produced by different erhus and thereby make the decision upon comparison. Just like other musical instruments, you should only trust the real item that you see IN PERSON. As such, I don't recommend buying an erhu from the Internet since you cannot try to play it before making the purchase.

In case you have nobody to rely on, there is still a simple way to judge its quality: push the bow against the inner string without pressing it, and then push the bow against the outer string by pressing it with the 3rd (ring) finger. These are aimed at finding whether there are any wolf tones or unpleasant sounds. If the sounds are soft and solid but not hoarse and rough, then the erhu should be qualified.

The erhus available in a music store should have already been assembled, yet if you by chance purchase an erhu of which the parts are separated (like those directly shipped from local manufacturers in China), you can bring the parts together with reference to the following chapter.

How to Set up an Erhu

To set up an erhu, take the following steps:

1)   Under most circumstances, the head, neck, sound box and tuning pegs are all connected.   In case the tuning pegs are separated, just plug them into their respective holes on the neck gently.   We can then assemble other parts in the following sequence: the strings > the bow > the bridge (together with the pad) > the nut.

2)   We usually install the inner string prior to the outer string. Before installation, we have to stretch the strings that are packed as a coil to restore them to a wire.   By doing so, you will discover that one end of the string is a small ring, while the other end is wrapped with nylon thread.

3)   Now pass the nylon-thread end through the small hole on the tuning peg, and wind the string around the peg.   Meanwhile, affix the ring end onto the screw for the inner string located at the bottom of the base, and slowly twist the tuning peg to fasten the string.

4)   Repeat the above process for the outer string save that we have to insert the bow hair between the strings, which means that the outer string also has to pass through the space in the midst of the bow hair and the bow stick.   Please refer to the video below for installing the strings: https://www.youtube.com/watch?v=Xo4abHfpxrc&t=56s

5)   When the strings are ready, we will install the bridge.   Slightly loosen the strings to allow enough space for the bridge to be positioned at the center of the snakeskin (where the pressure on the snakeskin is uniform), and fasten the strings again so that they adhere to the grooves

on the bridge. The bridge can be shifted slightly upward if the sound is dull or the snakeskin is loose; otherwise we will usually place it 0.5 mm above the center to reserve room for the pad beneath. Do not force the bridge to slide on the snakeskin lest that the latter would be damaged, and remember to loosen the strings each time to readjust the position of the bridge.

6)   Eventually we have to set the nut on the neck, which is conventionally 39 cm above the bridge. Nevertheless, this distance can change to cope with our palm size (i.e. the larger the palm, the longer the distance), and is roughly equal to the separation from the left elbow to the proximal phalange joint of the middle finger. For the way of typing the nut, please refer to the video below:
https://www.youtube.com/watch?v=N4ikTuNDOdA

7)   We have successfully set up the erhu. The above steps are visualized in the following schematic diagrams for easy reference:

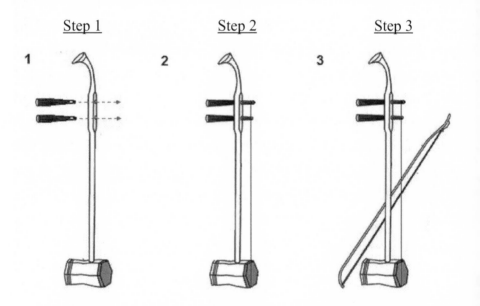

Step 4	Step 5	Step 6

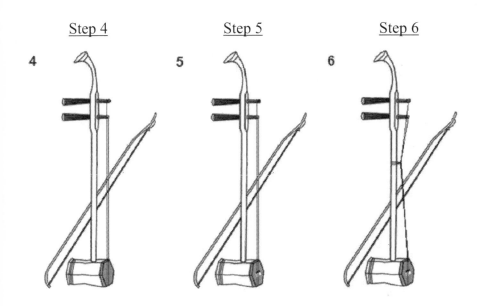

Step 2 – the two ends of an erhu string

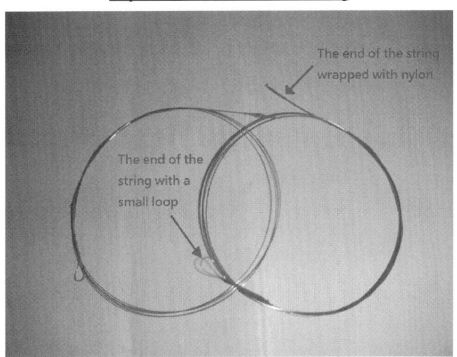

The end of the string wrapped with nylon

The end of the string with a small loop

22

Step 3 – the screws at the bottom of the erhu

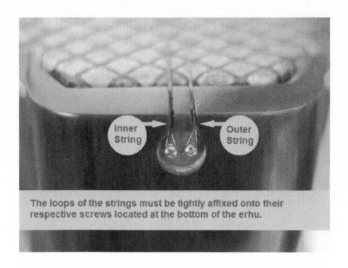

The loops of the strings must be tightly affixed onto their respective screws located at the bottom of the erhu.

On top of these, we can install a pair of "fine tuners" with which we can tune the strings slightly without twisting the tuning pegs.　They are not necessary, but are conducive to the tuning of the erhu.　Please refer to the video below for installing the fine tuners:

https://www.youtube.com/watch?v=ENOjo5hyJDg

Given that the string segments above the nut are wasted, attempts have been made to utilize these segments with a view to extending the range of the erhu, which gives rise to a new device called the movable nut. It is in fact an addition of another metallic nut on top of the original stringed-nut, which has been shifted upwards to render the extra tones by increasing the vibrating lengths of the strings.　Meanwhile, the movable nut can slide on the strings with its wheels such that the starting point of the open strings is altered.　Fine tuners are also equipped on the movable nut, which streamlines the process of tuning the erhu and changing its key signatures.　To be frank, the movable nut is extremely useful as many songs involve notes below D4, and we have to play these songs at the upper octave in order to maintain the

23

original key signature without the aid of such movable nuts. Therefore, I strongly recommend buying a movable nut and learn to use it skillfully.

Upon setting up the erhu, let's learn how to play the erhu.

How to Play the Erhu

We have to adopt the correct posture for playing the erhu. The traditional way is to sit on a chair, but some performers nowadays stand up or even walk while playing the erhu with the aid of a specially designed belt-clip. I personally prefer the sitting posture to those avant-garde postures, because many erhu maestros just sit on a chair to play the erhu. In this respect, I will introduce the traditional way:

1. Sit down and keep your back straight by occupying half of the seat only. You can either open or cross your legs (usually female players tend to cross their legs). Place the erhu on top of your left thigh (as shown in the picture below) and hold its neck with your left hand.

2.   Check whether both of the strings are tuned correctly with the aid of a tuner (the inner and outer strings at D4 and A4 respectively). Twist the tuning peg of the inner string clockwise and the tuning peg of the outer string anticlockwise to tighten the strings up for raising the pitches and vice versa (as shown in the pictures below).

 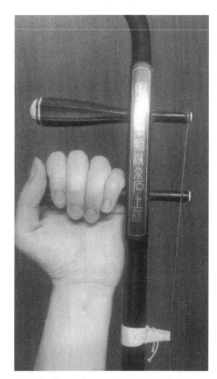

Twisting the tuning pegs for the inner string (left) and outer string (right)

3.   Loosen the screw device of the bow if the hair is too tight and vice versa (as shown in the picture below).   Don't fasten the hair too much and keep it slightly loosed.   Use your right hand to grip the bow with the thumb at the top, index finger next to the stick, middle and ring fingers between the stick and the hair, and little finger beneath the hair (as shown in the picture below).

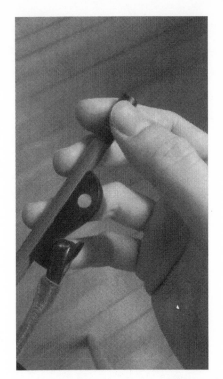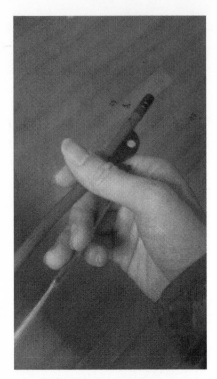

Adjusting the screw device (left) and gripping the bow (right)

4.   Gently push the bow outward and inward against either of the inner or outer string.   The angle between the bow and the neck should always be 90°, i.e. they are perpendicular to each other.   Without pressing any strings, the notes produced are D4 (inner string) and A4 (outer string), which are called the open strings.   Keep practicing the open strings until you no longer produce any hissing sounds like the crow of a cock being killed.   This process varies from person to person, but with enough efforts you should be able to overcome it within a month.

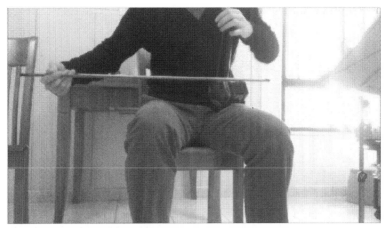

Pushing the bow to the right (down-bow)

Pushing the bow to the left (up-bow)

Afterwards, we can start playing some simple songs, though beforehand we have to learn to read the **numbered musical notation**, which is widely adopted in Chinese sheet music.

The Numbered Music Notation

The sheet music of the famous English folk song, *Green Sleeves*, is attached below for demonstrating how to read and interpret sheet music written in the numbered music notation:

Green Sleeves

English Folk Song

$1= C (2 6) \frac{3}{4}$ $\rfloor = 58$

6 | 1 - 2 | 3 - 4 3 | 2 - 7 | 5 - 6 7 | (5)

1 - 6 | 6 - #5 6 | 7 - #5 | 3 - 6 | (9)

1 - 2 | 3 - 4 3 | 2 - 7 | 5 - 6 7 | (13)

1 . 7 6 | #5 . #4 5 | 6 - 6 | 6 - 6 | (17)

5 - - | 5 . #4 3 | 2 - 7 | 5 . 6 7 | (21)

1 - 6 | 6 - #5 6 | 7 - #5 | 3 - - | (25)

5 - - | 5 . #4 3 | 2 - 7 | 5 - 6 7 | (29)

1 . 7 6 | #5 . #4 5 | 6 - - || 6 - 0 | (33)

The numbered music notation is based on the French Galin-Paris-Chevé system and known as *jianpu* (簡譜) in China. The sheet music for all Chinese musical instruments (including the erhu) is written in this notation, so we must learn to read it.

General principles

The numbered music notation gets its name because it uses numbers (0 – 7) to represent musical notes, but the numbers indeed tally with the solfeggi directly:

1 = do; 2 = re; 3 = mi; 4 = fa; 5 = sol; 6 = la, 7 = si/ti; and 0 = a rest irrespective of the key signatures of the sheet music.

The encircled areas in the above sheet music carry special meaning:

①: The name of the song "*Green Sleeves*" is located at the top;

②: The origin (/composer/ arranger) "*English Folk Song*" of the song is located at the top-right corner;

③: The key signature (1 = C), time signature (3/4) and tempo ($\mathcal{J}$ = 58) of the song are all located at the top-left corner;

④: The small number inside the bracket indicates the current bar number, which is the 5th bar in this case.

⑤: In Bar 33, the double bar lines marks the end of the sheet music. The bars are usually arranged in the order of a number's multiple (like there are 4 bars per line in this sheet music except the 1st line), but the actual arrangement depends on the number of notes present within a bar.   More notes will lead to fewer bars per line.

The key signature

The key signature is indicated by the expression 1 = X for majors and 6 = X for minors, though the minor notation is never used as far as I have observed.   This song is in the C major as indicated by 1 = C.

The numbers inside the brackets (2 6) indicates that the inner and outer OPEN strings will produce the solfeggi "re" (2) and "la" (6) of the C major.   The relationship between the majors and the solfeggi of the open strings is as follows:

Key Signature	Notation	Inner String	Outer String
D major	(1 5)	1	5
E ♭ major	(7 #4)	7	#4
E major	(♭7 4)	♭7	4
F major	(6 3)	6	3
G ♭ major	(#5 #2)	#5	#2
G major	(5 2)	5	2
A ♭ major	(#4 #1)	#4	#1
A major	(4 1)	4	1
B ♭ major	(3 7)	3	7
B major	(♭3 ♭7)	♭3	♭7
C major	(2 6)	2	6
D ♭ major	(#1 #5)	#1	#5

The octaves are represented by adding a dot above or below the number.   A dot below the number lowers the note by an octave, whereas a dot above the number raises the note by an octave.   For example, $\dot{1}$ is at an octave higher than 1 whereas $!$ is at an octave lower than 1.

The sharp (♯) sign raises the note by a semi-tone and the flat (♭) sign lowers the note by a semi-tone, whereas the natural (♮) sign neutralizes any sharps or flats from preceding notes or the key signature.

The time signature

The time signature is represented by fractions such as 2/4, 4/4, 6/8... which mean that there are 2 quarter notes per bar, 4 quarter notes per bar and 6 eighth notes per bar respectively. In this song, there are 3 quarter notes per bar as indicated by the fraction 3/4.

The tempo

The tempo, if any, will be written next to the time signature in the form of ♩ = X, which means that there are X quarter notes per minute. In this song, ♩ = 58 means that there are 58 quarter notes per minute. Sometimes, you may find a symbol ＋, which means "Ad libitum" (as you desire). Nonetheless, the tempo will vary as per the requirements of individual songs.

The note value

Underlined notes (like the solfeggio "6" in Bar 5) will have their lengths decreased by half per underline they have. On the contrary, notes followed by dots (like the solfeggio "1" in Bar 14) will have their lengths increased by half per dot they have. If they are followed by a hyphen (like the solfeggio "5" in Bar 5) instead of a dot, their lengths will be doubled.

Though absent in the above sheet music, dynamics (*p, f, mf, mp, ff, pp*), hairline crescendos and diminuendos will be written below the notes if necessary.

There are also erhu-specific marks that instruct us how to play the notes correctly. Musical symbols commonly found in erhu sheet music are tabulated below:

Relating to fingering technique

Symbol	Name	Meaning
⌐ or 0	Open string	Press no strings
— or ⌡	1st finger	Press the strings with the index finger
= or ⌐⌡	2nd finger	Press the strings with the middle finger
≡ or ⌐⌡	3rd finger	Press the strings with the ring finger
四 or ✕	4th finger	Press the strings with the little finger
↑ or ↗	Glissando (upward)	Glide the pitch upward slightly (left) and greatly (right)
↓ or ↘	Glissando (downward)	Glide the pitch downward slightly (left) and greatly (right)
↩ or ↪	Glissando (revolving)	Glide the pitch upward (left) or downward (right) and back to the original pitch afterwards

↑	Pressuring vibrato	Exert pressure on the strings to achieve the vibrato effect	
~~	Gliding vibrato	Perform glissandos of large amplitude to achieve the vibrato effect	
∞	No vibrato	Do not perform vibrato	
tr or tr~	Trill	Play the indicated note with its major second or others as specified in multiple rapid alternations. The wave after the "tr" sign lengthens its duration	
⋀⋀	Upper mordent	Play the indicated note with its upper major second or others as specified in a single rapid alternation	
⋀⋁	Lower mordent	Play the indicated note with its lower major second or others as specified it in a single rapid alternation	
O	Natural harmonic	Produce harmonics at natural harmonic points	
◊	Artificial harmonic	Produce harmonics at any but natural harmonic points	
⌐┘	Pizzicato (left hand)	Pluck the strings with the left hand (usually using the middle finger)	
+	Pizzicato (right hand)	Pluck the strings with the right hand (usually using the index finger)	

Relating to bowing technique

Symbol	Name	Meaning
內	Inner string	Push the bow against the inner string
外	Outer string	Push the bow against the outer string
⊓ or ⌐ (or)	Down-bow	Push the bow from the frog to the tip (to the right)
V or ∟ (or)	Up-bow	Push the bow from the tip to the frog (to the left)
⌢	Legato	Play all the linked notes within one bow stroke smoothly
⌢ⁿ	Multiplets	Divide a note into n subdivisions of equal length permitted by the time signature, usually existing in the form of a triplet
▼	Martelé	Push the bow with pressure and release it explosively
—	Staccato	Play the notes brokenly
▽	Spiccato	Bounce the bow lightly between the strings
⫻	Tremolo	Move the bow back and forth at the tip extremely rapidly
九	Ricochet	Throw the bow between the strings
5 1 ⫽	Double stop	Vibrate both of the inner and outer strings simultaneously
X	Bow-hitting	Hit the sound box with the tip of the bow stick

This list is not exhaustive, but should have included most of the marks we will encounter in erhu sheet music. Detailed explanation of how to employ all these techniques will be discussed in later chapters.

If you are able to read the above sheet music without any difficulties, we can move on to the next stage to begin practicing with our left hand: the fingering for different key signatures of the erhu.

The Key Signatures of the Erhu

As mentioned before, erhu sheet music only exists in majors, which in theory can be either one of the 12 majors from A to G. Nevertheless, we only play six of them (D, F, G, A, B♭ and C) with the erhu conventionally.

To know the reason, we can look into the relationship between the solfeggi and their corresponding notes for all 12 majors:

Key Signature	Note (in the ascending order of solfeggio)						
	1 (do)	2 (re)	3 (mi)	4 (fa)	5 (sol)	6 (la)	7 (ti)
A	**A**	B	C♯	**D**	E	F♯	G♯
B♭	B♭	C	**D**	E♭	F	G	**A**
B	B	C♯	D♯	E	F♯	G♯	A♯
C	C	**D**	E	F	G	**A**	B
D♭	D♭	E♭	F	G♭	A♭	B♭	C
D	**D**	E	F♯	G	**A**	B	C♯
E♭	E♭	F	G	A♭	B♭	C	**D**
E	E	F♯	G♯	**A**	B	C♯	D♯
F	F	G	**A**	B♭	C	**D**	E
G♭	G♭	A♭	B♭	C♭	D♭	E♭	F
G	G	**A**	B	C	**D**	E	F♯
A♭	A♭	B♭	C	D♭	E♭	F	G

Do you notice any patterns in the above table?

Since the inner and outer strings of the erhu are tuned at D4 and A4 by default, we naturally prefer those majors with both of the **D and A natural** notes.   With the D and A notes marked in bold type, it can be clearly seen that only the D, F, G, A, B ♭ and C majors have both of them. Therefore, traditional erhu songs are usually composed in the former six majors.

In view of this, we shall first learn to play the traditional six majors, which can be further divided into three groups according to the fingering within the 1st position:

1. The D, G and A majors that all start at the nut;

2. The F and B ♭ majors that both start further away (1.5 tones) from the nut;

3. The C major that usually starts at the 2nd position (the 1st position is usually used only if the solfeggi (3) and (4) are involved).

As such, we will practice the six majors in the order of D, G, A, F, B ♭ and C consequently (etudes will be provided for each major).

The D Major

The fingering for the five positions of the D major is shown below:

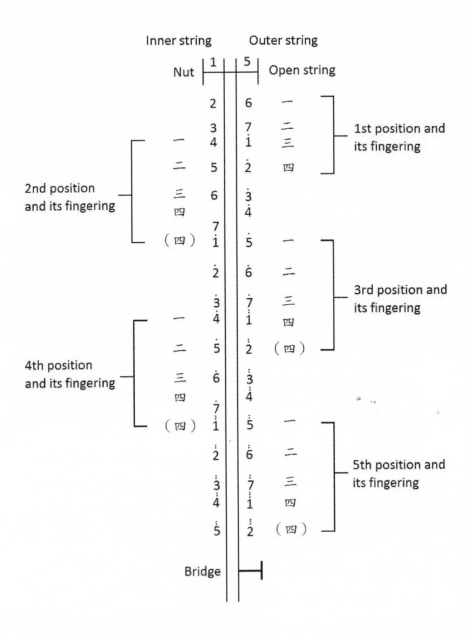

The D major is the fundamental major among all the majors, and we need to familiarize ourselves with it as a result. We shall focus on the 1st position to practice the scale from D4 to E5, and start from the open strings first:

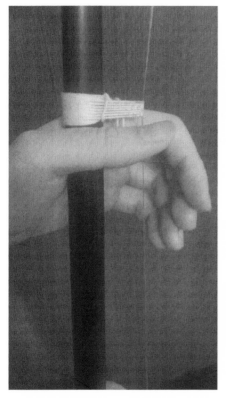 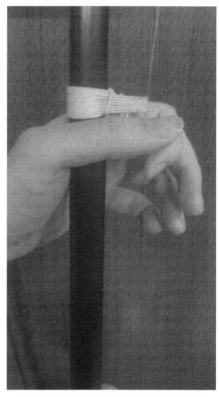

Pressing no strings will produce D4 (inner string) and A4 (outer string) notes, which are called the open strings.

Pressing the strings with the 1st (index) finger will produce E4 (inner string) and B4 (outer string) notes.

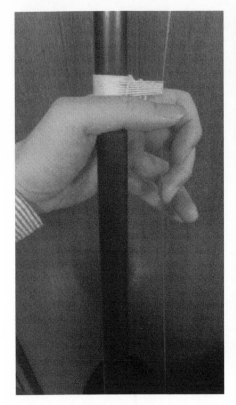 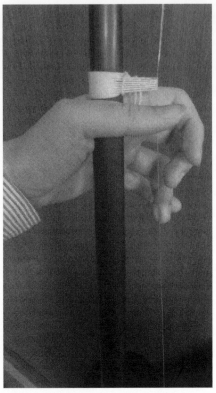

Pressing the strings with the 2nd (middle) finger will produce F♯4 (inner string) and C♯5 (outer string) notes.

Pressing the strings with the 3rd (ring) finger will produce G4 (inner string) and D5 (outer string) notes.

Since the F♯4/G4 and C♯5/D5 notes differ by a semitone only, the middle and ring fingers must stick together when we press the strings.

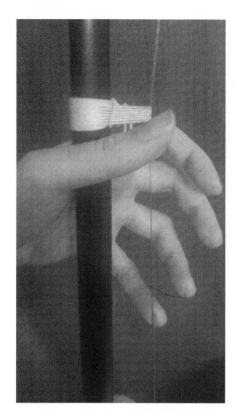

Pressing the strings with the 4th (little) finger will produce A4 (inner string) and E5 (outer string) notes.

Note: By extending the 4th finger downward, those solfeggi marked with (四) beside can be played without changing our left hand to the next position. This skill applies to all majors and is extremely useful when we play songs with a fast tempo by avoiding the movement of the left hand in changing positions.

It can be seen that either playing the outer open string or pressing the inner string with the 4th finger can produce the A4 note. Whether to produce the note from the inner or outer string varies from song to song, and the sheet music will often instruct us to push the bow against the desired string with the corresponding erhu-specific mark.

It is important to master the skill of changing positions; otherwise the notes we can play are limited. The erhu has around two and a half octaves, ranging from D4 to A6 (and a few notes over A6). The sound amplitude gradually diminishes as the pitch rises, and therefore we seldom play those notes beyond this range. At the elementary level, it is already enough for us to learn the 1st, 2nd and 3rd positions since the remaining two are less frequently used.

42

The fingering for the 2nd and 3rd positions is similar to that of the 1st position, and hence I only provide the photo of pressing the strings with the 1st finger within the 2nd position:

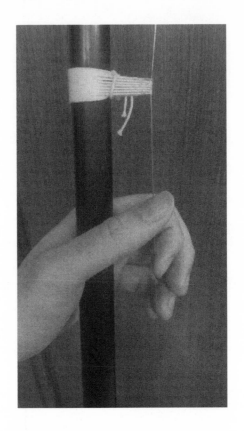

Please note that our fingers should become closer and closer when pressing the strings at higher positions, as the pitch is getting closer too. This phenomenon occurs in all majors, and hence it is better to practice the scales within different positions with the aid of a tuner.

Etude 1

1=D (1 5)

Moderato

$\frac{3}{4}$ 1 2 3 | 4 - - | 2 3 4 | 5 - - | 5 4 3 |

6 - - | 7 1 6 | 5 - - | 7 1 2 | 6 - - | 6 7 1 |

5 - - | 5 6 7 | 4 - - | 4 3 2 | 1 - - ‖

Etude 2

1=D (1 5)

Moderato

$\frac{2}{4}$ 5 1 | 6 3 5 | 1 5 6 3 | 5 - | 5 1 | 6 3 2 | 5 3 5 1 | 2 - |

3 2 | 3 5 6 | 7 6 7 5 | 6 - | 5 1 | 6 5 3 | 2 1 3 2 | 1 - ‖

Etude 3

1=D (1 5)

Moderato

$\frac{3}{4}$ 1 2 3 4 5 | 1 7 1 2 1 | 5 6 5 4 3 4 | 5 - - |

1 2 3 4 5 | 6 5 6 7 6 | 5 6 5 4 3 2 | 1 - - ‖

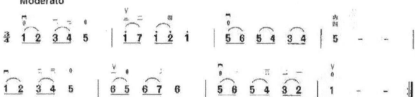

Etude 4

1=D (1 5)

Moderato

$\frac{4}{4}$ 3 2 3 4 5 6 5 4 | 3 2 3 4 5 5 | 4 3 4 5 6 7 6 5 | 4 3 4 5 6 6 |

5 4 5 6 7 1 7 6 | 5 4 5 6 7 7 | 6 5 6 7 1 2 1 7 |1. 6 5 6 7 1 1 ‖2. 6 5 6 7 1 1 ‖

44

The G Major

The fingering for the five positions of the G major is shown below:

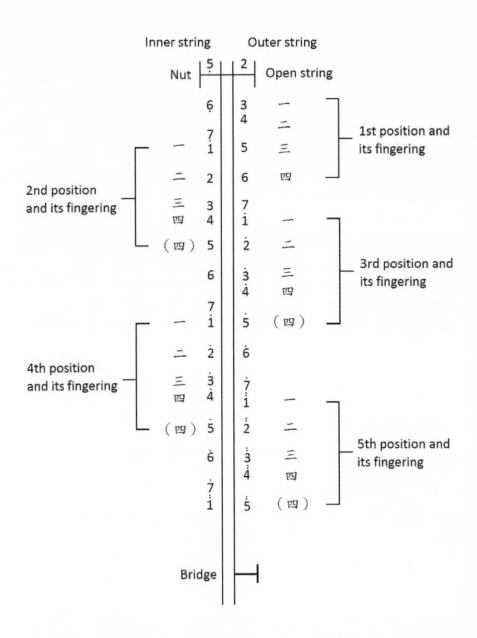

The G major is similar to the D major, except that the index and middle fingers must stick together when we press the outer string in the 1st position, as the notes B4/C5 are a pair of semitones.

When comparing the fingering charts of the D and G majors, we can discover that whenever we change the position, our index finger always start at the solfeggi "1" or "5". The pattern repeats itself at higher positions, and holds true for all majors that we are going to learn. However, in reality we will not abide by these fingering charts obstinately, but rather follow the instructions in every sheet music. Some teachers also perform songs in their own styles with tailor-made fingering. In this case, we should treat these fingering charts as a learning tool, but not a doctrine that we have to blindly obey.

Etude 1

1= G (5 2)
Moderato

Etude 2

1= G (5 2)
Moderato

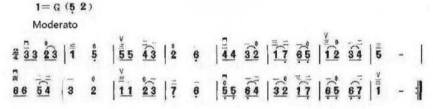

Etude 3

1= G (5 2)
Moderato

Etude 4

1= G (5 2)
Moderato

The A Major

The fingering for the five positions of the A major is shown below:

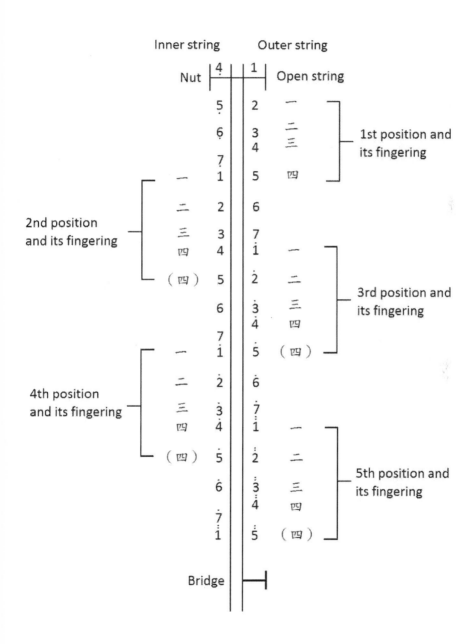

The A major is also similar to the D major, except that the ring and little fingers must stick together when we press the inner string in the 1st position as the notes G♯4/A4 are a pair of semitones.

Etude 1

1=A (4 1)
Moderato

2/4 5432 | 1. 3 | 2176 | 5 - | 4585 | 6712 | 3 1 | 5 - |

5432 | 3. 4 | 3217 | 6 - | 5543 | 2175 | 6 7 | 1 - ‖

Etude 2

1=A (4 1)
Moderato

2/4 3 3 32 | 1 5 | 5 5 54 | 3 1 | 2 3 45 |

4 3 | 2171 | 2 - | 44 43 | 2 6 | 33 32 |

1 5 | 45 67 | 12 34 | 54 32 | 3 - ‖ 1 - ‖

Etude 3

1=A (4 1)
Moderato

2/4 15 31 | 54 321 | 53 54 | 3212 3 | 15 31 |

54 231 | 55 43 | 2176 5 | 45 75 | 176 545 | 67 12 |

1.76 7 | 15 31 | 54 321 | 53 54 | 3215 1 ‖

Etude 4

1=A (4 1)
Moderato

6/8 54 345 2 | 43 234 1 | 32 123432 | 17 67 5. |

17 67 1 5 | 76 567 4 | 65 45 67 12 | 34 32 1. ‖

50

The F Major

The fingering for the five positions of the F major is shown below:

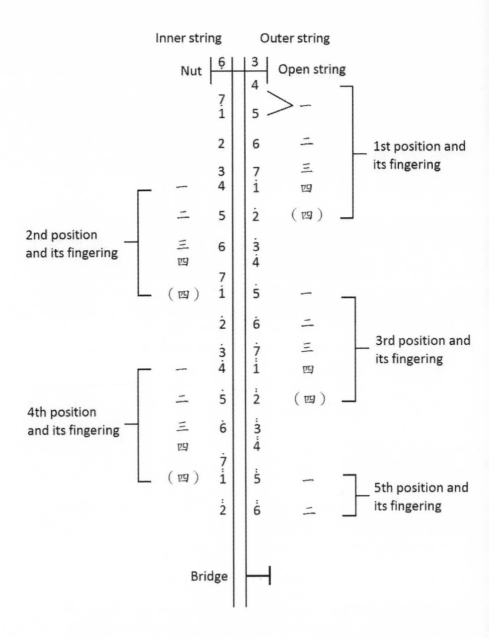

The fingering for the F major is a bit different from that of the D major, as we usually press the strings with the 1st (index) finger at a point below the nut for about 1.5 tones (as shown in the picture below).

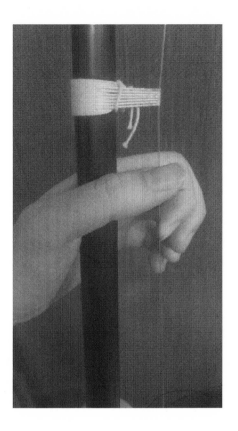

Note: We play the solfeggi (^{7}) and (^{4}) with the index finger in the 1st position as well.

Etude 1

1= F (6 3)

Moderato

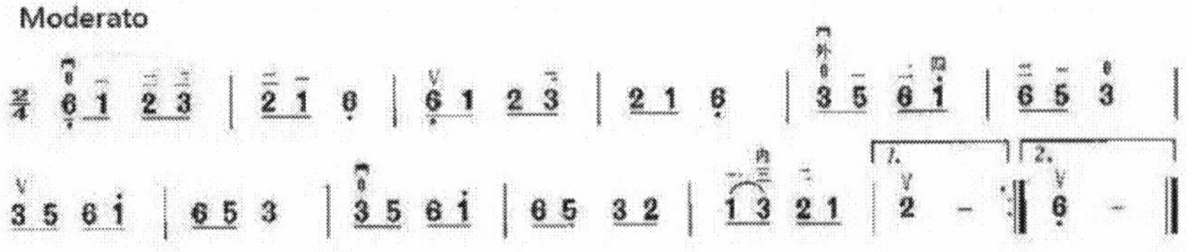

Etude 2

1= F (6 3)

Moderato

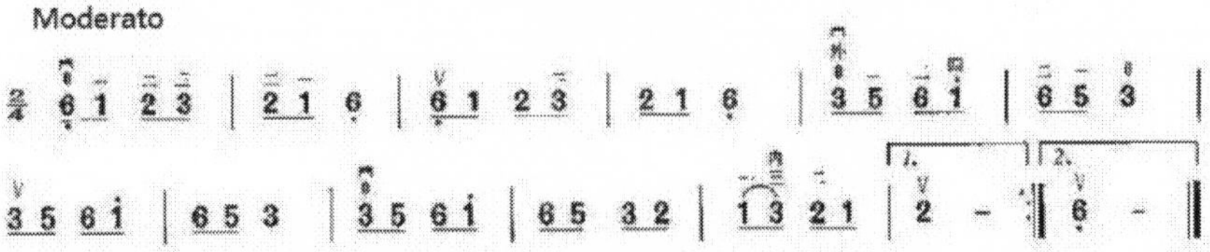

Etude 3

1= F (6 3)

Moderato

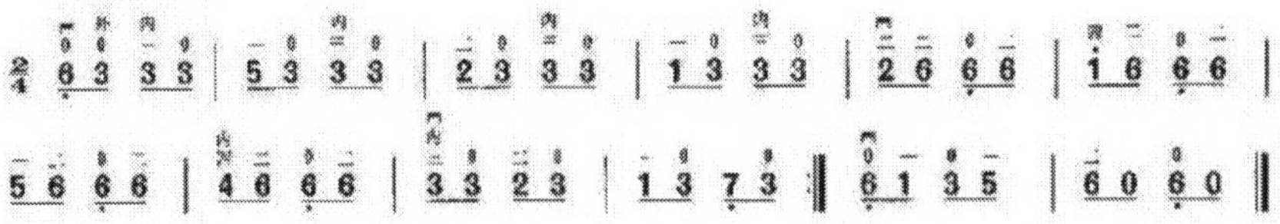

Etude 4

1= F (6 3)

Moderato

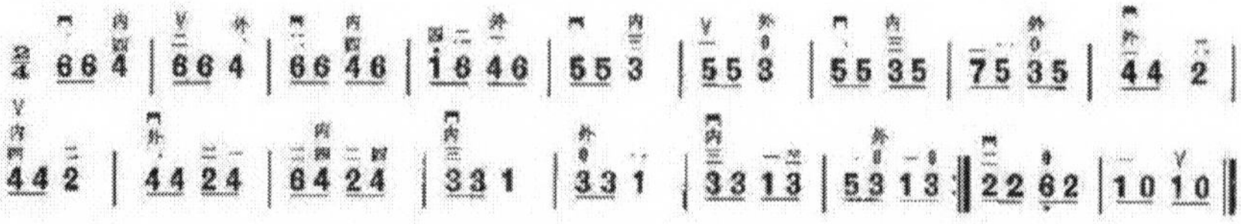

The B♭ Major

The fingering for the five positions of the B♭ major is shown below:

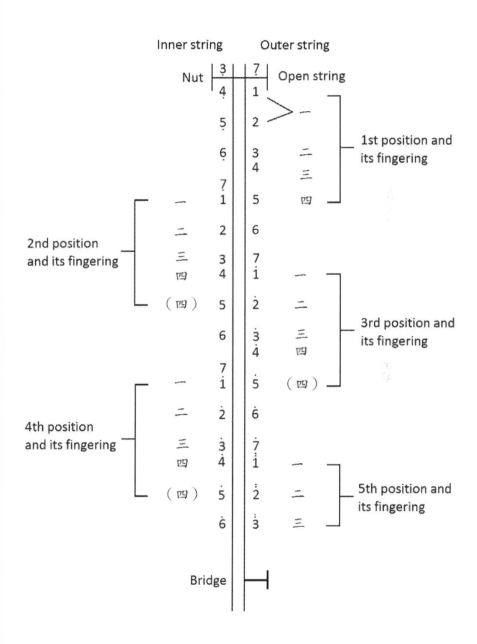

The B♭ Major is almost the same as the F major, except that the middle and ring fingers must stick together in the 1st position when we press the outer string as the notes D5/E♭5 are a pair of semitones.

Note: We play the solfeggi (4) and (1) with the index finger in the 1st position as well.

Etude 1

1=♭B (3 7)

Moderato

Etude 2

1=♭B (3 7)

Moderato

Etude 3

1=♭B (3 7)

Moderato

Etude 4

1=♭B (3 7)

Moderato

The C Major

The fingering for the five positions of the C major is shown below:

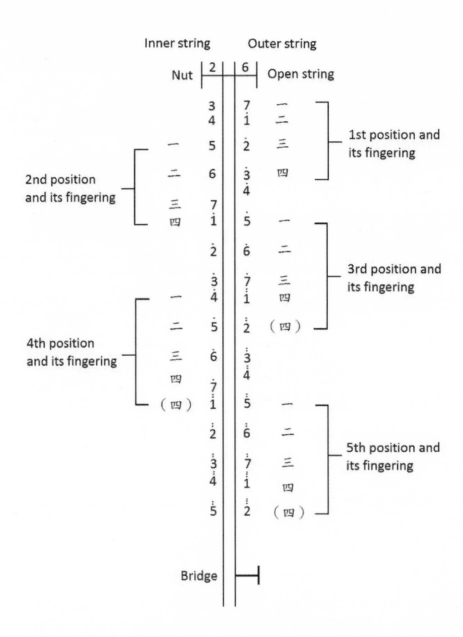

For the C major, we usually start at the 2nd position (as shown in the picture below) because the 1st position is used only if the solfeggi (3) and (4) are involved (the solfeggi in the 1st position are oddly arranged when compared with other majors).

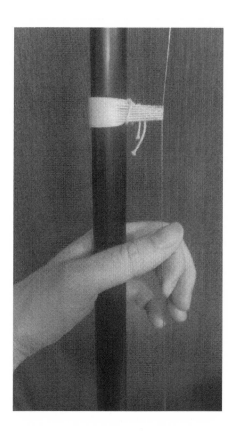

Etude 1

1= C (2 6)
Moderato

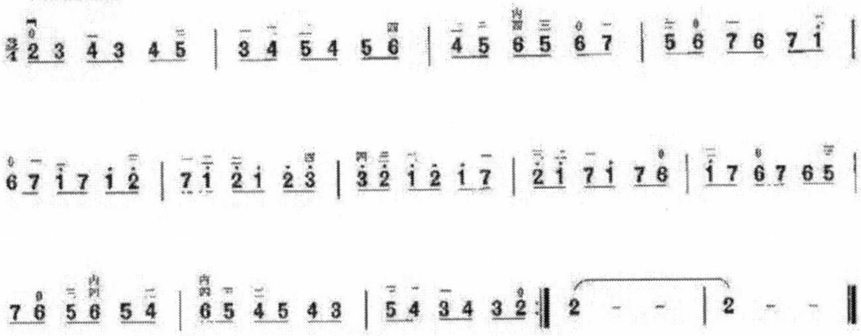

Etude 2

1= C (2 6)
Moderato

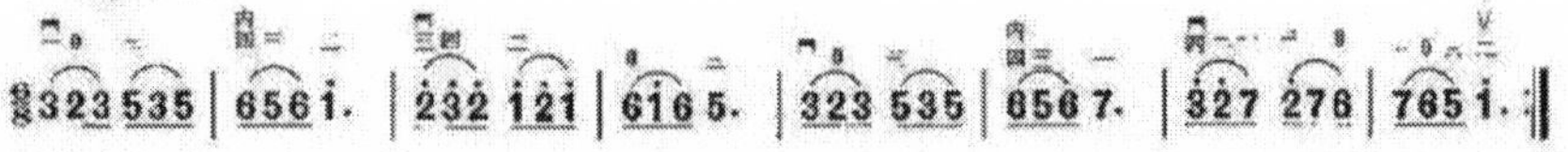

Etude 3

1= C (2 6)
Moderato

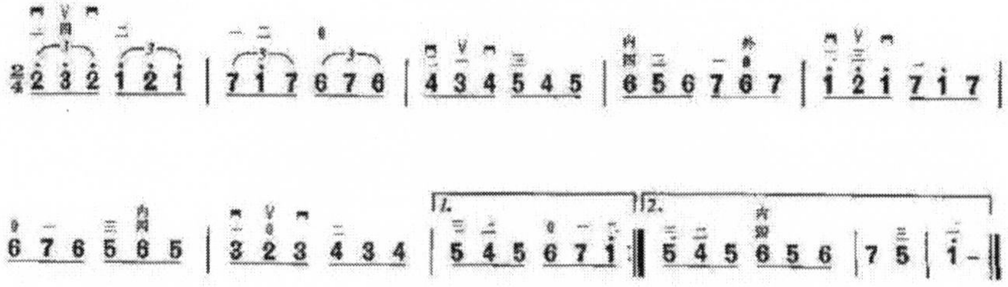

Etude 4

1= C (2 6)
Moderato

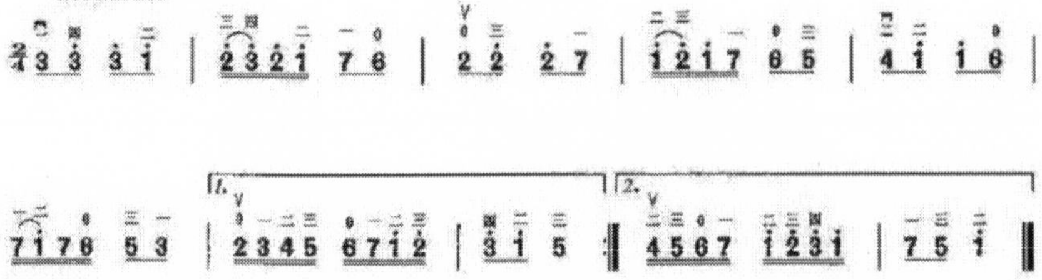

These six majors are what traditional music books and teachers will teach you; however, we should not be complacent about this. I used to be stuck on these majors, but soon discovered that many songs, especially pop songs or other adapted songs, are written in the remaining majors, which must be mastered if I want to play them with the erhu. Nevertheless, the solfeggi represented by the open strings under the remaining majors are often flatted or raised semitones, which is hard for us to tell them apart from their natural counterparts on the strength of our ears. Thus, we will sometimes mistakenly produce the natural notes with the open strings. I recommend practicing the scales of these majors with the aid of a tuner at the first place to make sure that all the notes are played at the correct pitches.

Among the remaining majors, the E and E♭ majors should be learnt by heart due to their frequent appearances; on the contrary, the G♭ major will not be introduced owing to its scarcity.

Likewise, we shall look into the fingering chart of each major, in the order of E♭, E, B, A♭ and D♭.

The E♭ Major

The fingering for the five positions of the E♭ major is shown below:

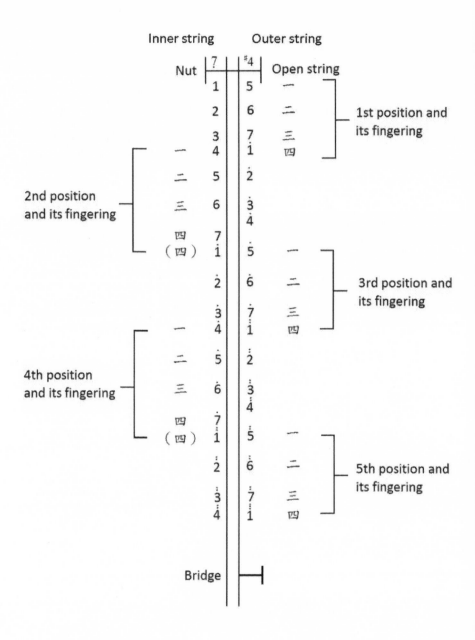

The E Major

The fingering for the five positions of the E major is shown below:

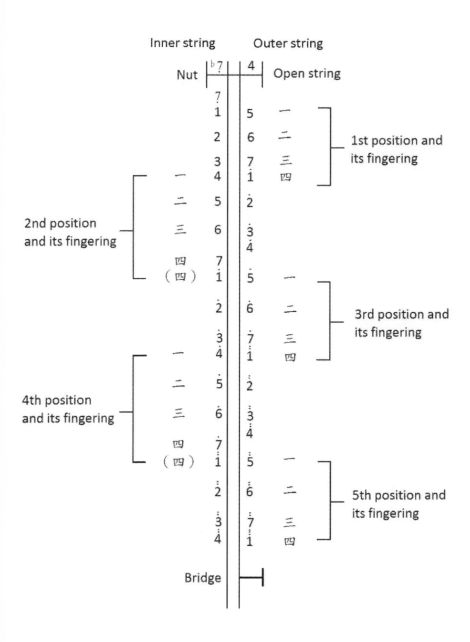

62

The E♭ major is actually similar to the D major, but only starts at a point below the nut for a semitone. We have to push the bow against the inner string and press it with the 4th (little) finger to render the A♭ note (4).

The E major is also similar to the D major, but starts at a point below the nut for a tone this time. Like the F and B♭ majors, we simply shift the 1st (index) finger upward to press the strings within the 1st position to render the D♯4 (7) note.

The above picture shows the starting point of the E♭ major. As the corresponding point for the E major is just a bit lower, I intend not to show its picture here in view of its subtle difference.

The B Major

The fingering for the five positions of the B major is shown below:

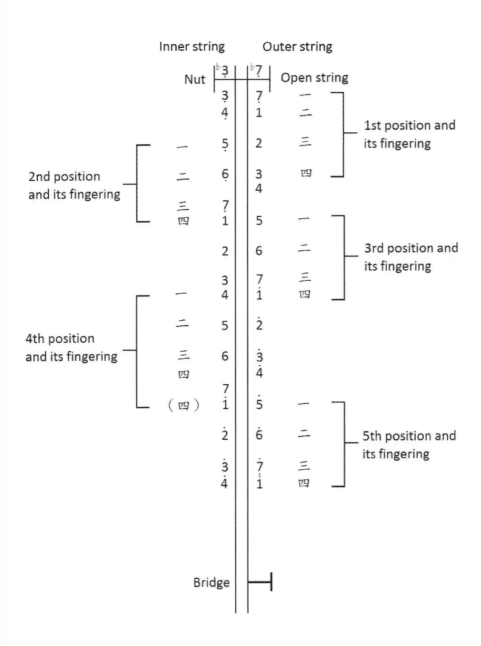

The B major is similar to the C major instead of the B♭ major, but we have to start at a point below the nut for about 2 tones (see the picture on the right), as compared with 2.5 tones for the C major. We can press the strings with the 1st (index) finger within the 1st position to render the natural solfeggi D♯4 and A♯4 ($\overset{.}{3}$, $\overset{.}{7}$).

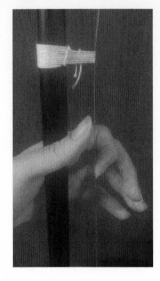

The A ♭ Major

The fingering for the five positions of the A ♭ major is shown below:

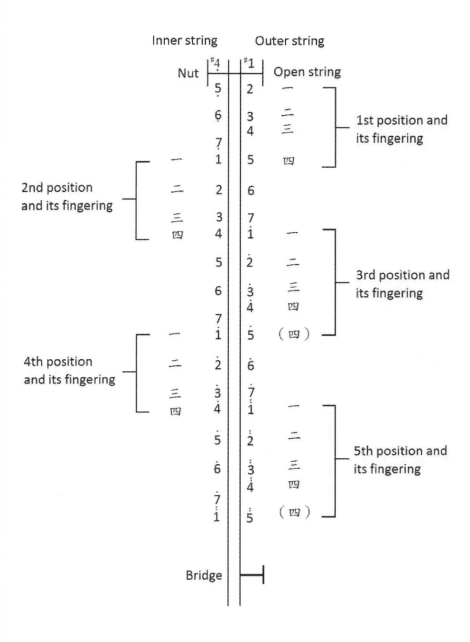

The D♭ Major

The fingering for the five positions of the D♭ major is shown below:

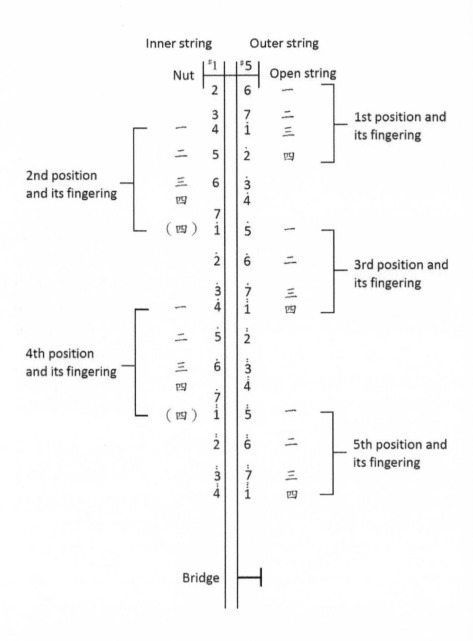

The A♭ and D♭ majors are almost identical to their natural counterparts save that the entire fingering is shifted upward to the nut for a semitone (see the picture on the left). In other words, the notes produced by pressing the strings with the 1st (index) finger and by the open strings are pairs of semitones.

If the key signature does not change throughout the whole song, i.e., remaining in the A♭ or D♭ majors, there is a simpler way to play the song: by tuning the strings at D♭4 and A♭4, we can apply the fingering of the D and A majors directly. We can tune the strings up to (D♯4/A♯4) and down to (C4/G4) at most, yet I personally do not prefer doing so because the strings resonate the best at D4 and A4, and they will break prematurely if we twist the tuning pegs too often. It is not difficult to replace the strings, but quite fussy or even embarrassing if we do not have any spare strings with us.

Having acquired all the 11 majors, it is time for us to further sharpen the skills with both of our hands – the fingering (left hand) and bowing (right hand) techniques.

The Fingering Techniques

The major kinds of skills involving the use of our left hand include:

Glissando

Glissando, originating from the French word *"glisser"*, means the gliding of notes from a pitch to another pitch. Glissandos are child's play for string instruments like the erhu as their notes are continuous but not discrete (unlike the piano and other keyboard instruments).

To produce a glissando, press the strings at a note from which our finger glides upward or downward to another note. The range of glissandos can be within a tone (slightly upward/ downward) or exceed several tones (greatly upward/ downward). If the range is too large, we have to change the position at the same time to allow flexibility.

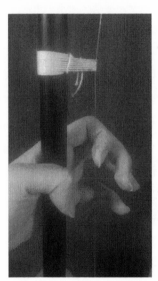

Sometimes, we glide our finger upward/ downward and return to the original note to produce several glissandos consecutively. This is known as revolving glissando, of which the range is usually within two tones.

The 1st finger glides from a lower note to a higher note to produce a glissando

Vibrato

Vibrato, an Italian word meaning "vibrated", is crucial to the timbre of all string instruments. Vibrato animates plain notes, transforming them into lively notes, as if a dead person were revivified, whose heartbeat changes from a straight line to a pulse.

————————————————————— A note without vibrato

 A note with vibrato

The ways to apply vibrato on the erhu depends on the types of vibrato concerned, which consist of rolling vibrato, pressuring vibrato and gliding vibrato. The rolling vibrato is the basic type and most commonly used. To do so, we need to train our left hand to wobble in the vertical plane without holding the neck of the erhu first. Shake our left hand vertically in a relaxed manner without holding anything. Then, hold the neck of the erhu and shake the hand in the same way. Push the bow against either of the strings slowly, and the rolling vibrato for the open strings has been done.

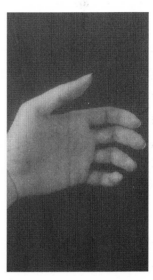

Shake our free left hand vertically in a relaxed way

We can subsequently press the strings with different fingers, and shake the whole left hand EXCEPT the finger in contact with the strings (which will vibrate with our left hand negligibly) this time. Don't slide the finger along the strings, or else the note will be out of tune.

70

Another type of vibrato is called the pressuring vibrato. To do so, we flex and extend the 2nd joint of our finger in contact with the strings to adjust the pressure exerted thereon, hence achieving an effect similar to the rolling vibrato. The pitch resulted is jagged and the sound is not smooth, yet it is suitable for expressing sadness and indignation.

The final type of vibrato is called the gliding vibrato. To do so, our finger glides over the strings to vary the vibrating length and the pitch subsequently, either in the upward or downward direction, in which the sounds generated differ a bit from the other types.

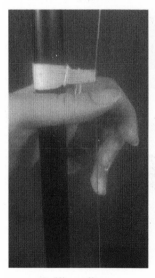  

Rolling vibrato	Pressuring vibrato	Gliding vibrato
The wrist vibrates sideways	The wrist remains static	The palm vibrates vertically

Vibrato is the most effective for long notes at a slow tempo, and less noticeable for short notes at a fast tempo, in particular when we need to change positions frequently.

We should always apply rolling vibrato, which will not be specifically marked, to all notes unless there are the no-vibrato marks or other instructions on the sheet music (like the pressuring vibrato or gliding vibrato marks).

Trill

The trill involves rapid alterations of two adjacent notes, usually a major second apart.

The above definition speaks for itself: we play a note with the principal finger and its major second with the auxiliary finger alternatively at a fast pace. The principal finger can be the 1st, 2nd or 3rd finger, whereas the auxiliary finger will be 2nd, 3rd or 4th finger (1st finger for the open strings). We can also produce a trill by alternating with other specified notes (like a major third), but the combination tends to be the 1st and 3rd fingers in this case.

The length of a trill is confined by the note but not by the length of the bow. We can play a trill with several bow strokes, in which the alternations of notes usually take place faster and faster.

The 1st (index) and 2nd (middle) fingers act as the principal and auxiliary fingers respectively

The mordent, another fingering technique, is similar to the trill save that the alternation of notes only occurs once, while alternations of notes recur for the trill. If the auxiliary note is lower than the principal note, we call it the lower mordent; otherwise we call it the upper mordent.

Harmonic

In physics, the term "harmonic" refers to a series of tones relating to the fundamental tone in terms of their frequencies; in music, the fundamental tone is the lowest note a musical instrument can produce. As for the erhu, the fundamental tone refers to the D4 (inner) and A4 (outer) notes of the open strings because the full vibrating lengths of both strings have been utilized.

Tones with frequencies as integer multiples (2, 3, 4, 5...) of the frequency of the fundamental tone are called overtones. By definition, the fundamental tone is the 1st harmonic, whereas the 1st overtone is the 2nd harmonic. We call these harmonics *the natural harmonics* because they fall within the category the physical laws.

The name of the overtone denotes its number of overtones, i.e. the 2nd overtone has 2 overtones, whereas the 3rd overtone has 3 overtones. There are unlimited overtones in theory, but we only count up to the 4th overtone for the erhu since overtones beyond it do not sound well and are seldom employed in reality.

The following diagram lists the fundamental tone along with the 1st to 4th overtones of the erhu. The intersections where the overtones meet are the points at which we can produce the natural harmonics.

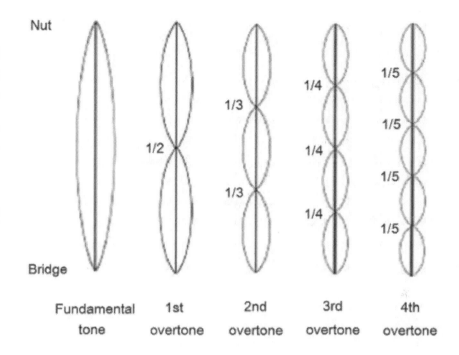

Nut

1/3

1/4

1/5
1/5

1/2

1/3

1/4

1/4

1/5

1/4

1/5

Bridge

| Fundamental tone | 1st overtone | 2nd overtone | 3rd overtone | 4th overtone |

For better illustration, the relationship between harmonics, overtones and their corresponding notes for the erhu is tabulated as follows:

Harmonic	Overtone	Note (Inner string)	Note (Outer string)
1st harmonic	Fundamental tone	D4	A4
2nd harmonic	1st overtone	D5	A5
3rd harmonic	2nd overtone	A4, A5	E5, E6
4th harmonic	3rd overtone	G4, D5, D6	D5, A5, A6
5th harmonic	4th overtone	F♯4, B4, F♯5, F♯6	C♯5, F5, C♯6, C♯7

According to the wave equation $v = f \bullet \lambda$ (wave speed = frequency x wave length), the wavelength (so as the vibrating length) is inversely proportional to the frequency. Thus, we need to press the strings at 1/2, 1/3, 1/4, 1/5 and 2/5 of the full vibrating length accordingly (as shown in the picture below) to produce the overtones.

	Inner string			Outer string	
	D4			A4	
Overtone	Actual tone	Position		Actual tone	Overtone
F#6	F#4	1/5		C#5	C#6
D6	G4	1/4		D5	A6
A5	A4	1/3		E5	E6
F#6	B4	2/5		F5	C#7
D5	D5	1/2		A5	A5
F#5	F#5	2/5		C#6	C#7
A5	A5	1/3		E6	E6
D6	D6	1/4		A6	A6
F#6	F#6	1/5		C#7	C#7

The harmonics of the erhu are crystal clear and transparent, like the sounds of a bell. In order to produce natural harmonics, we need to touch the strings at any of the aforesaid natural harmonic points GENTLY and push the bow against the desired string RAPIDLY with force, such that the bow hair grips the string as far as possible when moving against it. If you press the strings instead of touching them, the actual tones will be produced rather than the overtones.

Aside from the natural harmonics, we can also manually produce harmonics at any points we want, which are called *the artificial harmonics*.

While the full vibrating length for the natural harmonic is measured from the nut to the bridge, the full vibrating length for the artificial harmonic is measured from the 1ST (INDEX) FINGER to the bridge. By pressing the strings at any point with the 1st finger strongly and at the upper 1/4 or 1/3[7] of the remaining vibrating length with the 4th finger lightly, we can produce the perfect fourth or perfect fifth[8] artificial harmonic respectively, which will be two/ one and half octaves above the actual notes we play.

In the above picture, we substitute the 1st finger for the nut to produce the perfect fourth harmonic, with the overtones being D6/A6 at the inner and outer strings respectively

As we can press the strings with our 1st finger at any point, we can produce numerous artificial harmonics; yet pragmatically, we can only produce the perfect fourth and perfect fifth artificial harmonics up to B6/F7.

---

[7] Theoretically, we can also produce artificial harmonics at 1/2, 1/5 and 2/5 of the remaining vibrating length. However, given the short distance between our 1st and 4th fingers, it is impossible to produce harmonics at 1/2 and 2/5, and rare to produce harmonics at 2/5 in the case of the erhu.

[8] A perfect fourth and a perfect fifth consist of 5 and 7 semitones respectively.

The following tables summarize all the plausible artificial harmonics:

Perfect fourth artificial harmonic (inner string)

1st finger note	E4	F4	G4	A4	B4
4th finger note	A4	B♭4	C5	D5	E5
Harmonic produced	E6	F6	G6	A6	B6

Perfect fourth artificial harmonic (outer string)

1st finger note	B4	C5	D5	E5	F5
4th finger note	E5	F5	G5	A5	B♭5
Harmonic produced	B6	C7	D7	E7	F7

Perfect fifth artificial harmonic (inner string only; outer string is not used in this case)

1st finger note	E4	F4	G4	A4	B4	C5	D5	E5
4th finger note	B4	C5	D5	E5	F5	G5	A5	B5
Harmonic produced	B5	C6	D6	E6	F6	G6	A6	B6

For easy reference, the natural harmonics in terms of solfeggi for the six traditional key signatures of the erhu are depicted in the following diagram:

Natural Harmonics of the Erhu (in terms of solfeggi)

Position ratio
of the strings ←

	1 = D		1 = F		1 = G		1 = A		1 = Bb		1 = C	
	1	5	6	3	5	2	4	1	3	7	2	6

Position ratios (top to bottom): 1/5, 1/4, 1/3, 2/5, 1/2, 3/5, 2/3, 3/5, 3/4, 4/5

Overtone

Nut

Bridge

78

Pizzicato

Pizzicato, an Italian word meaning "pinched" or "plucked", is a rather interesting technique for bow-stringed instruments like the erhu, since it can produce sounds that are distinct from those produced by using the bow.

Using the left hand or right hand with any finger can do pizzicato, but we usually pluck the strings with the 2nd finger (left hand) and the 1st finger (right hand).   Let me explain how we pluck the strings with the right hand first.

Normally, we only pluck either of the inner or outer string at a time as we need to push the bow against the other string to facilitate the plucking action, whereby producing a clear plucked sound.   In the meantime, we can also press the strings in order to render the correct notes.   For instance, when plucking the inner string, we push the bow against the outer string WITHOUT moving it (as we do not mean to produce sounds by pulling the bow), and then pluck the inner string in the inward direction (facing us) with the 1st finger of our right hand. This process holds true for plucking the outer string, except that we pluck it in the outward direction (away from us).

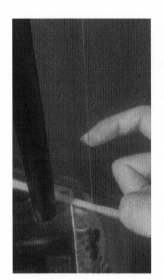

Pluck the inner string with the 1st (index) finger of our right hand

Pluck the inner string with the 2nd (middle) finger of our left hand

As for left-hand pizzicato, it is rather difficult since we need to press and pluck the strings concurrently. In fact, we can consider it an addition of a plucked sound prior to the principal note. Under most circumstances, we pluck the open strings with the 2nd finger of our left hand, yet occasionally we are required to pluck the strings with any of the remaining fingers. We should therefore practice more for plucking the strings smoothly.

We have concluded most of the fingering techniques, and will now carry on to the bowing techniques that involve the use of our right hand.

The Bowing Techniques

Even though we simply push the bow from the tip to the frog (up bow) or vice versa (down bow) most of the time, there are other bowing techniques we can employ as well, including:

Legato

Legato, an Italian word meaning "tied together", tells us to play all the linked notes within one bow stroke and minimize the silence between them.

It is actually the simplest technique (excluding down bow and up bow). When we see notes linked by a slur or tie[9] in erhu sheet music, we should always play them with a FULL bow unless the tempo is fast. Very often, we can reinforce it with vibrato to further enhance the smoothing effect.

Martelé

Martelé, a French word meaning "hammered", is done by pushing the bow against the string with pressure, holding the bow for a very short instant and then releasing it explosively. By varying the tension on the bow hair with our right hand, pulses of elastic notes with rests are produced when the bow moves against the string.

---

[9] A slur links notes of different pitches while a tie links notes of the same pitch.

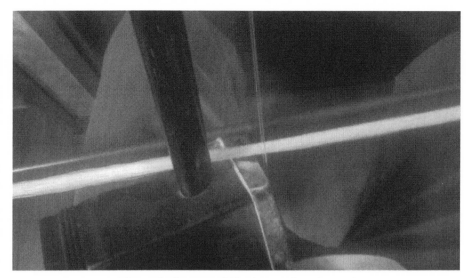

The explosive martelé is about to be triggered

The duration of notes with martelé is indeed reduced by half to allow time for the rests between them. So how can we produce martelé? The answer depends on which string we are referring to.

As for the outer string, we need to whirl our right hand clockwise dexterously like turning a screwdriver, by which the thumb and the middle finger will exert a force on the bow, making the bow hair adhere to the outer string when the bow moves against it.

As for the inner string, we need to press the bow hair with our middle and ring fingers in order to make it adhere to the inner string when the bow moves against it.

In both cases, we need to stop pushing the bow at the moment when a sound is generated. Relax our right hand such that the bow hair loosely touches the string, and thereupon we finish a martelé successfully.

Staccato

Staccato, an Italian meaning "detached", is similar to martelé that notes are shortened and separated by rests.

The only discrepancies between them are that the duration of notes with staccato is longer than that of martelé and staccato requires a constant force in the right hand.   As the silence between notes with staccato is achieved merely by stopping the bow without varying the tension on the bow hair, we have to maintain a stable force in our right hand throughout the course of staccato.

Spiccato

Spiccato, an Italian word meaning "separated", is the production of quick notes by bouncing the bow between the strings.

Spiccato is also similar to martelé, but the duration of notes is even shorter with a larger degree of springiness.   Unlike martelé, we usually apply spiccato to quick notes over phrases, preferably at the outer string due to the difficulty in controlling the quality of sounds at the inner string.

To produce spiccato, we grasp hold of the bow with the thumb, the index and middle fingers.   Choose a point for the bow to bounce, which will be closer to the tip of the bow for a faster tempo, or closer to the middle of the bow for a slower tempo.   Raise the bow a bit from the sound box and relax our right wrist.   Exert the pushing force on the bow from the upper arm by pivoting on the midpoint of the forearm. The bow will bounce between the strings accordingly thanks to the unconstrained motion of our right hand.

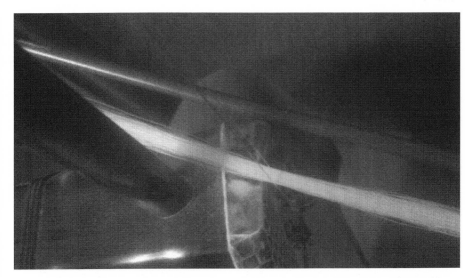
The bow hair should bounce between the inner and outer strings in spiccato

Bear in mind that our wrist should only move in the horizontal plane and not in the vertical plane, and that the bow hair should bounce between the strings inward or outward instead of upward or downward.

Tremolo

Tremolo, an Italian word meaning "trembled", is the rapid reiteration of a single note by pushing the bow back and forth against the strings briskly. In fact, it is equivalent to playing thirty-second notes (1/32) repeatedly. We can vary the intensity of the tremolo (in terms of the pushing force on the strings) to express different moods. For instance, a weak tremolo depicts a serene and vast atmosphere, whereas a strong tremolo depicts a lively and vigorous atmosphere.

The bow speed of tremolo is the fastest among others, and we do not count the exact number of notes in tremolo. Adjusting the position of the bow against the string, which is weaker at the tip and stronger at the middle, can vary the intensity of tremolo.

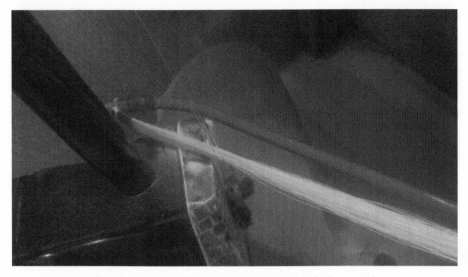

The bow usually vibrates the strings at the tip in tremolo

Like spiccato, we need to relax our right wrist as much as possible and exert the pushing force from the upper arm. By pivoting on the forearm, force will be transmitted to the hand, which leads to its dynamic motion in the horizontal plane. Tremolo is the most effective at fast speed, and therefore we must push the bow fast enough while maintaining it in a plane parallel to the sound box. However, bear in mind that we have to relax our wrist throughout the course of tremolo as a wrong posture during practices and performances will impair our right hand and even lead to permanent injury.

Ricochet

Ricochet, the throwing of the bow between the strings, is usually restricted to a few numbers of songs. It bears a resemblance to the stomping by horse hoof and consists of two parts: a short staccato before the bow is thrown, followed by several staccatos when the bow falls down.   In order to perform a ricochet, we first start with a down-bow or up-bow to produce a staccato.   Then, raise the bow to a certain height above the sound box with the forearm, and throw the bow to the space between the strings in the opposite direction of the previous bow stroke. When the bow is about to fall on the sound box, slightly relax the thumb and the index finger as well as press the bow hair downward with the middle and ring fingers to prevent the bow from rebounding upward. Consequently, several staccatos will be produced at the string against which the bow is thrown.

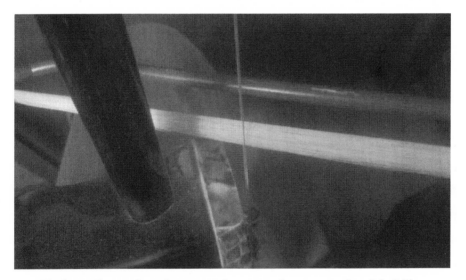

The bow vibrates the strings to produce several staccatos when it is falling

The bow hair should be tightened with our right hand to enhance the elasticity of the bow.   To get the best result, we need to choose the best bouncing point, which is closely related to the tempo.   Akin to spiccato, the point will be closer to the tip for a faster tempo, or closer to the middle of the bow for a slower tempo.

As a single ricochet only lasts for a very short period of time, the number of playable notes is limited, generally two to three notes.   Hence, we should emphasize the first note produced after the bow is thrown since the remaining notes are weaker in amplitude.

The key to a successful ricochet depends on the rotational motion rather than the vertical motion of the arm, yet an overdone vertical motion will adversely curtail the number of notes produced by a ricochet. There are also several minor mistakes that will hinder the success in producing a ricochet: 1) the fingers do not collaborate timely when the bow falls down; 2) the bow is raised too much; 3) noise is produced when the bow is raised; and 4) noise is produced when the bow stick hits the sound box.

Double Stop

This technique mimics the double stop of the violin, in which both the inner and outer strings are bowed simultaneously, but by different approaches as follows:

1) Tip up the bow stick and press the bow hair towards the sound box with the middle and ring fingers of the right hand. The bow hair will be flattened in the horizontal plane and can vibrate both strings at the same time. The effect by this approach is the best but the volume of sound generated is low;

2) While vibrating the inner string with the bow hair, we utilize the bow stick to vibrate the outer string at the same time. This approach will work only with tremolo or quick short bow strokes of which the pushing force is strong enough to produce substantial sound at the outer string. As such, the sound generated is a bit noisy; and

3) Quickly vibrating the inner and outer strings alternatively to create an illusion of double stop due to persistence of hearing.

87

The stick and hair vibrate the outer and inner strings respectively during a double stop

Bow hitting

In normal situations, hitting the sound box with the bow stick should be avoided as far as possible, yet it can also generate special sounds that certain songs desire. To do so, raise the bow frog slightly and hit the rear part of the sound box (near the window) with the bow tip, instead of the front part of the sound box (near the snakeskin) because the resonance effect is better at the rear. We have to exercise caution in hitting the sound box to prevent unnecessary noise arising from the contact with the strings.

Hit the rear part of the sound box with the tip of the bow stick to produce sounds

Neck bending

The lowest possible note the erhu can produce is D4, which is not even sufficient for songs that merely consist of the middle C (C4). Normally, when we encounter notes that are below D4, we will shift the whole song up by an octave if we want to maintain the song in its original key signature. However, there is indeed a special technique called 彎柱法, meaning "bending the neck" in English, that can lower the lowest note of the erhu by a minor third (three semitones) to B3.

Invented by WANG Shuliang (王曙亮) in 1962, the technique of "neck bending" is represented by the symbol ([) and performed as follows:

We first hold the neck with our left hand except the thumb, which is parallel to the neck instead. Make sure that the base does not slide on our thigh, and then exert force on the neck such that it slightly bends to the right side. By doing so, the distance between the tuning pegs and bridge becomes shorter, and thereby the strings loosen while their tension decreases. As a result, the pitch will also decrease.

Notable examples of songs employing this technique are *Resentment of the Pipa* (琵琶怨) and *Love of the Noble Consort* (貴妃情). In the last but one chapter of *Resentment of the Pipa*, the key signature is 1 = D but the lowest note B3/ solfeggio (6̣). There is actually no method to play these notes under normal circumstances, and only by applying the technique of neck bending, we can manage to play them.

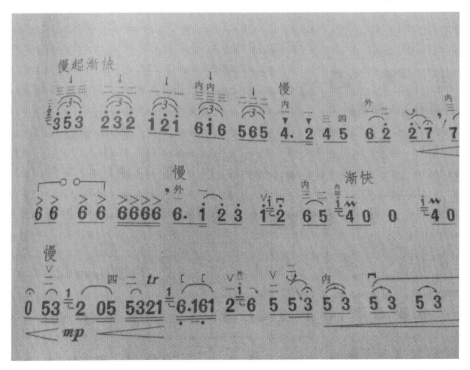

The above picture is extracted from *Resentment of the Pipa* (琵琶怨), and the neck bending sign [can be spotted on the solfeggi (6̣) in the third line

Attention: This technique will damage the junction of the neck and the sound box. Please use it at your own risk, especially for expensive erhus like those made of red sandal woods.

With regard to this hazard, we should seek another way to effectively lower the fundamental tone of the erhu without damaging any of its parts, and in fact there is a safer and more convenient way to achieve the same effect even to a greater extent – the utilization of a movable nut, by which we can permanently alter the tunes of both open strings while the erhu will remain intact.

Special Types of Erhus and Alternative Open Strings

Throughout the above chapters the erhus I introduce are all tuned at D4/A4 for the inner and outer strings, which is the default setting. However, there are indeed a few songs in the traditional realm in which the open strings are set at different pitches, and two notable examples are *Er Quan Ying Yu*/二泉映月 and the Great Wall Capriccio/長城隨想曲. I am not going to discuss the two songs in details since they are very difficult in nature, but want to highlight that the open strings for these songs are tuned at G3/D4 and C4/G4 respectively. In this connection, there are strings (*Chang Cheng Xian*/長城弦) and even erhus (*Er Quan Hu*/二泉胡) specifically designed for them (Having said that, we still employ the D-major fingering chart when playing both of these songs.)

The *Chang Cheng Xian*/長城弦 are thicker and harder than normal strings and can be directly installed on normal erhus to render the open strings as C4/G4 without relieving their tension so as to lower the pitches.

The *Er Quan Hu*/二泉胡 has a larger and flatter sound box than normal erhus, and its snakeskin is also thicker than usual. Equipped with longer strings, its full and effective vibrating lengths are also longer such that the open strings are tuned at G3/D4. A comparison of the parameters of a normal erhu and the *er quan hu* is shown below:

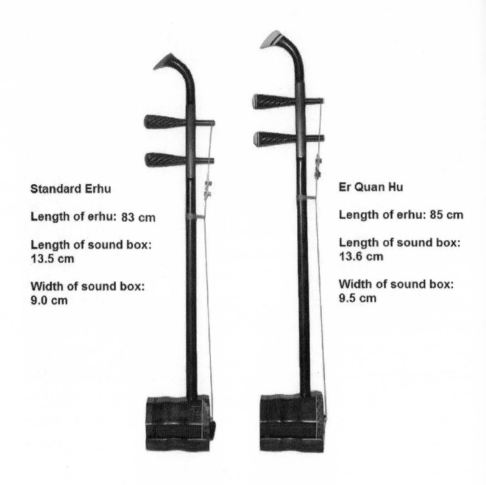

Standard Erhu

Length of erhu: 83 cm

Length of sound box: 13.5 cm

Width of sound box: 9.0 cm

Er Quan Hu

Length of erhu: 85 cm

Length of sound box: 13.6 cm

Width of sound box: 9.5 cm

The *er quan hu* (right) is apparently a larger version of the normal erhu (left)

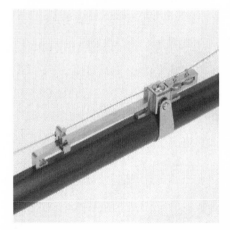

We can utilize the *Chang Cheng Xian*/長城弦 and *Er Quan Hu*/二泉胡 to play other songs aside from these two songs. Perhaps it is quite costly to purchase another erhu or troublesome to install another pair of strings, so we can manipulate the aforesaid movable nut to achieve a similar effect.

For instance, we shift the movable nut upward from the original D4/A4 to A3/E4 along its axis as shown in the right picture, in which the effective vibrating length of both strings increases and the pitches of the open strings become lower in turn. The A3/E4 setting is sufficient enough for us to play many adapted songs with the extra three notes (A3, B3 and C3) given. Notwithstanding, any notes between A3/E4 and D4/A4 can be chosen as the starting point of the nut at will.

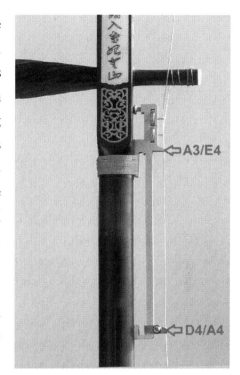

For the sake of simplicity, I will list the respective fingering charts under the new settings of opening strings (A3/E4, C4/G4 and G3/D4) in the following table:

Normal Erhu	Equipped with movable nut	*Chang Cheng Xian*/長城弦	*Er Quan Hu*/二泉胡
Fingering chart under the D4/A4 setting	Fingering chart under the A3/E4 setting	Fingering chart under the C4/G4 setting	Fingering chart under the G3/D4 setting
A	D	A♭	E
B♭	E♭	A	F
B	E	B♭	G♭
C	F	B	G

D♭	G♭	C	A♭
D	G	D♭	A
E♭	A♭	D	B♭
E	A	E♭	B
F	B♭	E	C
G♭	B	F	D♭
G	C	G	D
A♭	D♭	A♭	E♭

To utilize the above table, simply find out which fingering chart is to follow after changing the pitches of the open strings. For example, under the E major for the normal erhu, the lowest playable solfeggio is "7". If a song includes "5", we have to play the whole song an octave above if we have to retain it in the E major. However, if we use the movable nut, the corresponding fingering chart will be the A major with "4" as the lowest playable solfeggio. Hence, we can play the song without raising the octave.

It is worthwhile to mention that zhonghu/中胡 and gaohu/高胡 are tuned at G3/D4 and G4/D5 respectively. You can try to play them with respect to the above table if you have understood the principle behind the tuning mechanism.

Apart from all the above information, it is important to know the ways of maintaining the erhu, repairing damaged parts, as well as some accessories necessary for the erhu to function well.

Maintenance of the Erhu

The *Stradivarius* instruments have been made for several hundred years, but still function well thanks to the wonderful workmanship of their craftsmen, the prestigious *Stradivari* family. However, proper maintenance certainly plays a vital role in it.

Erhus can hardly be preserved for hundreds of years like violins due to the collapse of snakeskin, which will definitely take place after dozens of years upon its production, provided that it is used in an appropriate manner. This is, of course, already sufficient for us to make use of it. It is not easy to find a suitable erhu, and therefore we should properly maintain our erhu to prolong its usable life.

Different parts of the erhu require different ways of maintenance, which will be introduced with respect to each part as follows:

The head/ neck/ sound box/ base

The erhu is vulnerable to sunlight and moisture because its wooden parts will crack under strong sunlight and become mildewed if they get wet, and thus we should abstain from playing the erhu in the sun or rain. If the erhu accidentally gets wet, we must wipe it with tissue paper and dry it with a hair dryer (cool air) immediately.

As for storage, we should store the erhu in a dark and cool place with good ventilation. Someone prefers to hang the erhu on the wall, but I prefer to store it in the case lest that the erhu would fall on the ground inadvertently. To offer better protection to the erhu, place some mothballs in the case to repel insects that will eat the wood or the snakeskin.

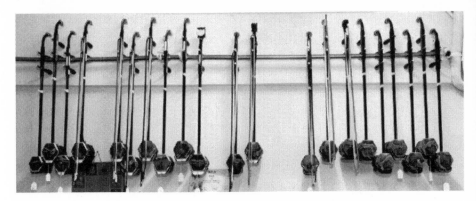

Erhus are hung on the wall in a typical musical store

The snakeskin

The snakeskin is the soul of the erhu, so we need to pay extra attention to its care. Interestingly, the snakeskin will undergo several stages in its life, and different approaches should be adopted to cater for its specific needs at different stages.

For a newly made erhu, the snakeskin is tightly affixed to the sound box by the crafter, resulting in a sharp and crackling timbre. At this stage, we need to play the erhu more often to customize the snakeskin. When time passes, the snakeskin will resonate better.

After a few years, the snakeskin should have become "mature", which means that it has coped with other parts at the optimum level. At this stage, we should keep playing the erhu to further customize the snakeskin, and consider taking some protective measures:

The first measure is to relieve the pressure exerted by the bridge on the snakeskin. Under normal circumstances, both the inner and outer

97

strings are tightly fastened, which exert a great pressure on the bridge that in turn transmits the pressure to the snakeskin, accelerating the collapsing process. To counteract the pressure, we can loosen the strings, raise the bridge to an upper position near the edge of the snakeskin, or put a small cylinder of wood above the bridge.

By loosening the strings, we directly reduce the pressure exerted on the bridge and hence the snakeskin. However, we have to twist the tuning pegs to readjust the tension on the strings whenever we want to play the erhu. Not only the strings are prone to break due to frequent changes in tension, the tuning pegs and their respective holes on the neck will also abrade gradually. It is easy to replace the strings, but very hard to find another pair of identical tuning pegs. As a result, I do not recommend loosening the strings.

Someone prefers to raise the bridge upward until they reach the edge of the snakeskin, where the pressure will be diverted to the sound box. Similarly, the frequent changes in the position of the bridge will damage the snakeskin due to the abrasion between the surfaces. Worst still, the bridge cannot be raised unless the strings are loosened.

Raising the bridge can significantly reduce the pressure on the snake skin, and hence slow down the collapsing process

In this respect, I don't recommend raising the bridge unless you are not going to play the erhu for a long period of time. In such a case, you can even remove the bridge (see the picture on the left) and store it elsewhere, by which the strings have no contact with the snakeskin, and all pressure will be eliminated at once.

Personally, I would rather prefer placing a small cylinder of wood, which can be a ready-made snakeskin protector available in musical stores or the internet, or a pencil cut into half on our own, above the bridge as a substitute to divert the pressure. Whenever we finish playing the erhu and put it back into the case, we can place the cylinder of wood above the bridge and remove it when we play the erhu again.

You can purchase a specially designed snake skin protector like the one shown in the picture above to divert the pressure

The second measure is to maintain the humidity because it has a significant impact on the snakeskin, which will expand when it is hot and humid, and contract when it is cold and dry. Despite the difficulty in maintaining a constant temperature and humidity all the time, we should strive to store the erhu in a relatively stable environment. It may be costly to control the temperature, so we will seek to control the humidity instead.

Someone suggests applying vegetable oil, Vaseline or even wax to the surface of the snakeskin, but neither of these should be encouraged as the grease will dampen the snakeskin and affect the sounds. In fact, the snakeskin is more hydrophobic than hydrophilic in nature, and high humidity will expedite the collapsing process.

We should therefore aim at dehumidifying the snakeskin by placing some desiccants or a dehumidifier in the case.

The bow

The bow can be acquired at a low cost, but we can still do something to prolong its life. Whenever playing the erhu, we must rub the bow hair with rosin, which increases the friction between the bow hair and strings, and fosters better vibrations. For a newly purchased bow, we should apply more rosin to the bow hair to prevent its breakage due to the pushing action without sufficient amount of rosin. If there is little hair left, the bow cannot vibrate the strings well (like producing distorted and cracking sounds), we should purchase another bow, or just replace the bow hair if the bow stick is made of expensive materials. Please refer to the video below for rubbing the bow with rosin and fitting the bow between the strings:

https://www.youtube.com/watch?v=qygR2KE12jY

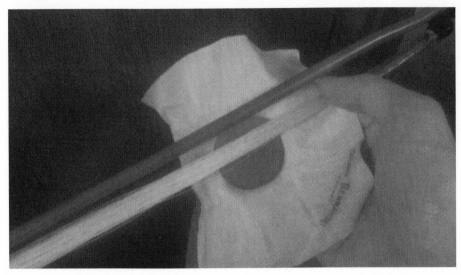

Rub the bow hair with rosin evenly to increase its friction with the strings

The strings

A pair of new inner and outer strings of the erhu available in the market

The strings are susceptible to breakage owing to frequent playing and rusting over time. Moreover, the strings are always stretched under normal tuning setting, which will cause them to become fatigue and lose strengths. The outer string is in particular more vulnerable because it is thinner than the inner string.

When the strings break or no longer produce the correct tones, we need to replace them.

The nut

Type the loops of nut again when the rope-typed nut breaks (mainly due to moisture, especially palm sweat).

Other accessories

Rosin

The rosin for violins can be directly applied to erhus, so there is no need to put much effort in finding one for the erhu.

Rosin serves to facilitate the string vibrations by increasing the friction with the bow hair, but excessive rosin powder will disperse on the erhu, where they will stick to the wood and affect the sound produced.

Thus, we should apply optimum amount of rosin before playing the erhu, and remember to immediately remove all the rosin powder accumulated on it with a clean cloth afterwards, because after a long time they cannot be wiped out unless chemicals are used. For instance, we can add a few drops of oil to melt the rosin, but beware of any oil spilt over the bow hair or snakeskin for oil is detrimental to them.

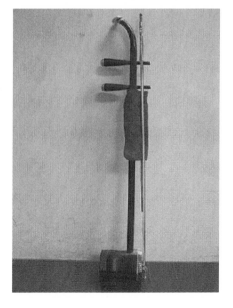

When storing the erhu in its case, we can also wrap the strings with a long piece of cloth to separate them from the bow hair to prevent the rosin powder from being glued to the strings.

Corner piece

Subject to daily abrasion from the bow hair, the corner piece will gradually wear out. We should replace it with a new one, which can be affixed on the original position by using super glue.

At last, the syllabus for the graded examination of the erhu from Grade 1 to Grade 10 (Performance Certificate) is attached herewith for the purpose of practices. If you are interested to sit for the above examination, you should keep practicing these songs until you can play them skillfully.

Selected Erhu Etudes and Songs for Central Conservatory of Music Practical Examination (Grade 1 to Grade 10)

中央音樂學院音樂水平等級術科考試
二胡考級曲目（第一至十級）

Grade 1

A) Etude
1、第一把位 D、G、F 調七聲音階 　　　　　　　　　劉長福曲
2、換弦交替指練習 　　　　　　　　　趙寒陽、劉逸安曲
3、D 調三、四指音準校正練習 　　　　　　　　　王曙亮曲
4、連弓練習 　　　　　　　　　劉長福曲

B) Song
1、田園春色 　　　　　　　　　陳振鐸曲
2、簫 　　　　　　　　　蘇北民歌
3、鳳陽花鼓 　　　　　　　　　安徽民歌
4、迷胡小曲 　　　　　　　　　豐芳曲
5、西藏舞曲 　　　　　　　　　西藏民歌
6、長城謠 　　　　　　　　　劉雪庵曲

C) Oral
1、概述 　　　　　　　　　肖學俊
2、樂曲分析 　　　　　　　　　肖學俊
3、音樂基礎知識測試例題 　　　　　　　　　翁建偉

Grade 2

A) Etude
1、上把位指距練習 　　　　　　　　　宋國生曲
2、中把位綜合練習 　　　　　　　　　王國潼編曲
3、快弓練習 　　　　　　　　　劉長福曲
4、切分弓法練習 　　　　　　　　　劉昌盧曲

B) Song
1、小花鼓 　　　　　　　　　劉北茂曲
2、黃水謠 　　　　　　　　　冼星海曲 蔣巽風訂弓指法
3、沂蒙山小調 　　　　　　　　　山東民歌 張銳編曲
4、窗音 　　　　　　　　　內蒙古民歌 王志偉訂弓指法
5、快樂的校園 　　　　　　　　　孫奉中曲
6、春雨 　　　　　　　　　王壽庭曲

C) Oral

1、概述 肖學俊

2、樂曲分析 肖學俊

3、音樂基礎知識測試例題 翁建偉

Grade 3

A) Etude

1、琶音與分解和弦練習 劉長福曲

2、F 調換把練習 趙寒陽曲

3、指序練習 劉德海編曲

4、快速換弦練習 張澤倫曲

B) Song

1、山村變了樣 曾加慶曲

2、良宵（除夜小唱） 劉天華曲

3、賽馬 黃海懷曲 沈利群改編

4、喜唱豐收 楊惠林、許講德曲

5、拉駱駝 曾尋編曲 張韶訂弓指法

6、新農村 曾加慶曲

C) Oral

1、概述 肖學俊

2、樂曲分析 肖學俊

3、音樂基礎知識測試例題 翁建偉

Grade 4

A) Etude

1、C 調力度練習 劉逸安、趙寒陽曲

2、兩手配合練習 周耀錕曲

3、快速換把練習 王國潼曲

4、A 調把位音準練習 王志偉曲

B) Song

1、光明行 劉天華曲

2、奔馳在千里草原	王國潼、李秀琪曲
3、喜送公糧	顧武祥、孟津津曲
4、趕集	曾加慶編曲
5、北京有個金太陽	藏族民歌 蔣才如編曲

C) Oral

1、概述	肖學俊
2、樂曲分析	肖學俊
3、音樂基礎知識測試例題	翁建偉

Grade 5

A) Etude

1、固定音型換弦練習	馮志皓曲
2、活指換弦練習	趙硯臣曲
3、綜合練習	宿英曲 居文鬱改編
4、兩手配合練習	劉長福曲

B) Song

1、翻身歌	張頡誠曲 王國潼編曲
2、空山鳥語	劉天華曲
3、燭影搖紅	劉天華曲
4、陝北抒懷	陳耀星、楊春林曲
5、流波曲	孫文明曲 項祖英訂弓指法

C) Oral

1、概述	肖學俊
2、樂曲分析	肖學俊
3、音樂基礎知識測試例題	翁建偉

Grade 6

A) Etude

1、長弓練習	閔惠芬曲
2、D 大調練習	(法)克萊采爾曲
3、換弦與指距練習	王國潼曲

4、快弓與轉調練習 劉長福曲

B) Song

1、葡萄熟了 周維曲

2、江南春色 朱昌耀、馬熙林曲

3、月夜 劉天華曲

4、江河水 東北民間樂曲 黃海懷移植

5、聽松 華彥鈞曲 曹安和記譜
儲師竹 、黎松壽擬訂指法

C) Oral

1、概述 肖學俊

2、樂曲分析 肖學俊

3、音樂基礎知識測試例題 翁建偉

Grade 7

A) Etude

1、琶音綜合練習 趙硯臣曲

2、查爾達什（片段） (匈)蒙蒂曲

3、小二度音程模進練習 趙寒陽曲

4、五聲音階模進與轉調練習 劉長福曲

B) Song

1、春詩 鍾義良曲

2、豫北敍事曲 劉金文曲

3、草原新牧民 劉長福曲

4、洪湖人民的心願 張敬安、歐陽謙叔原曲
閔惠芬編曲

Grade 8

A) Etude

1、快速大跳練習 劉長福曲

2、固定唱名記譜轉調練習 周耀錕曲

3、五聲音階練習 趙硯臣曲

| 4、純八度練習 | 趙寒陽曲 |

B) Song

1、秦腔主題隨想曲	趙震宵、魯日融編曲
	張韶修訂弓法
2、三門峽暢想曲	劉文金曲
3、二泉映月	華彥鈞傳播 楊蔭瀏記譜
	儲師竹、黎松壽擬訂指法
4、病中吟	劉天華曲

Grade 9

A) Etude

1、綜合練習	劉長福曲
2、自然音程大跳練習	趙寒陽曲
3、霍拉舞曲	羅馬尼亞民間舞曲
	選自王國潼、周耀錕、張韶編
	選的《二胡練習曲選》（續集）
4、增二度音程練習	趙寒陽曲

B) Song

1、一枝花	民間樂曲 張式縠改編
	蘇安國訂弓指法
2、藍花花敍事曲	關銘曲
3、新婚別	張曉峰、朱曉谷曲 閔惠芬
4、長城隨想（二胡協奏曲主旋律譜）	劉文金曲

Performance Certificate

A) Etude

1、轉調與綜合練習	劉長福曲
2、音樂會練習曲	周耀錕曲
3、無窮動（D調片段）	[意]帕格尼尼曲 嚴潔敏移植
4、八度音程練習	趙寒陽曲

B) Song

1、陽光照耀著塔什庫爾幹　　　　　　陳鋼編曲　劉天華移植
　　　　　　　　　　　　　　　　　鄧建棟訂弓指法
2、第一二胡狂想曲　　　　　　　　　　　　　王建民曲
3、流浪者之歌　　　　　　[西]薩拉薩帝曲　選自張韶著
　　　　　　　　　　　　　　《二胡廣播教學講座》
4、貴妃情　　　　　　　　　　　　　　　盧亮輝曲

Online Materials

For more information about the contents of this book, please visit my blog at https://howtoplaychinesemusic.blogspot.hk/
and my YouTube channel at
https://www.youtube.com/channel/UCf2mOLx4wonalASaSbnpWJg

Thank you very much!

41211842R00068

Made in the USA
Middletown, DE
04 April 2019